*Journey to Joy*

# Journey to Joy

The Story of

Norman and Marie Ens

*Marie Ens*

Christian Publications

CAMP HILL, PENNSYLVANIA

*Christian Publications*
*3825 Hartzdale Drive, Camp Hill, PA 17011*

*The mark of* ✝ *vibrant faith*

ISBN: 0-87509-555-0
LOC Catalog Card Number: 93-74547
© 1994 by Christian Publications
All rights reserved
Printed in the United States of America

94 95 96 97 98   5  4  3  2  1

Cover illustration
© 1994, Karl Foster

# Dedication

———

I fondly dedicate this book
to my grandchildren—

Tyler Blaine Ens Sylvester
Kristie Marie Ens Sylvester
Allesha Janelle Plastow Ens
Jesse Mark Pak Ens
Ellen Elizabeth Weilenman Ens
Andrew Benjamin Plastow Ens
Adam Benjamin Ens Sylvester
Stephanie Ruth Pak Ens
Oliver Weilenman Ens
James Melvin Ens Sylvester

As they walk the paths of their lives in obedience to our
Lord Jesus, may they experience even greater blessings
than those they read of here.

# Contents

# 1

# A Dream Come True

First-termer. The very word indicates inexperience, ineptitude, ignorance and numerous other uncomplimentary characteristics.

But that's what we were—first-termers!

Our initiation into missionary life in Cambodia was diligently supervised with care and affection by David and Muriel Ellison who made it their personal concern that we apply ourselves industriously to language study and become quickly integrated into the exciting work of sharing the gospel. It was fortunate for us that they did so, for in just 10 short months a family emergency called the Ellisons home and we were left on our own.

We began our ministry in the little village of Kompong Speu. We were young. We had a new country. We had a new home. We had a new baby, our third, and we had a new ministry. It was exciting—the fulfillment of our dreams.

Our home was a large, wooden house built on pillars. The walls were one board thick, painted bright blue on the side that faced the narrow, dirt road. But the inside was unpainted and the wood floors, also unpainted, were waxed to a high gloss. Big windows, actually only openings, were barred to keep out thieves and screened to keep out mosquitos but allow any small breeze to enter unhindered.

Water was ingeniously pumped from a well in the garden to a huge metal tank placed in the attic of the house. We enjoyed in Cambodia what we never had in our Canadian pastorate—running water. The cold showers were just what we needed in such a climate.

The large garden boasted 12 kinds of fruit, including limes, oversize green bananas, little yellow finger bananas, pineapples, guavas, pomegranates and more.

To a town overflowing with brown-skinned, dark-eyed, black-haired people we brought our chubby, blue-eyed towhead—Douglas Paul. Wherever we went he was besieged by admirers. His amah (babysitter) adored him. And his parents? Well, to his mother every morning felt like Christmas when she awoke to remember he was there.

>─┼─◀▶─◉─◀▶─┼─◀

This new life and ministry was the realization of our dreams. We were finally missionaries!

The dream for me actually began in 1934. Peter and Justina Engbrecht had been in Canada just seven years after immigrating from a Mennonite village in Russia. The Great Depression had left them financially poor but it had not been able to diminish their spirit. With faith and the ingenuity born of poverty they were managing to provide for their six children—four boys and two girls.

Food was simple—great slices of fragrant, homemade white bread and fresh vegetables from the huge garden that Justina diligently planted, weeded, watered and harvested each year.

Sunday the menu was different. There was always a treat to celebrate that special day. Justina's children were sure she made the best sugar cookies in all of Saskatchewan.

Clothes were practical, most of them handmade for the children by their mother from bright, store-bought material, but more often from flower sacks or used clothing recycled for the next generation.

Except Sunday. Then everyone dressed up to walk the short distance to the big, German-language Mennonite Church.

Life after seven years in a new country had taken on a certain routine for the Engbrecht family. In his carpenter shop built onto the house next to the kitchen Peter worked hard to support his family. Money was scarce for everyone and payment took many forms—perhaps a pail of lard, a few eggs or some farm produce.

Justina cooked and sewed and cared for three-year-old Irene while the other children attended the village school. In the winter, with the sun barely visible as it slid over the horizon, they would arrive home famished, kick off galoshes and snowsuits and slide into their places on the rugged bench beside the big kitchen table.

Yes, life was pretty routine in the Engbrecht household.

Then one day Justina had to face an inescapable fact—she was pregnant. Again! She struggled against accepting another baby. Weren't six children an ample brood to provide for in these tough times? With all but one child now in school wasn't she just beginning to enjoy a certain amount of freedom?

It took a while, but with the arguments and rationalizations finally set aside, Justina was able to bend her will to God's will. As the baby grew within her Justina had a private, unspoken desire known only to the Lord—a desire she whispered again and again to Him and Him only.

In October of 1934, in the upstairs bedroom of their humble home, Justina and Peter's seventh child was born. It was a girl. That made four boys and three girls.

Justina thought her prayer could only be answered through a son. Now she had a daughter. Perhaps that was why she had not dared to share her secret longing with anyone.

If Justina was disappointed she never showed it. Her baby girl was enveloped in an abundance of tender love. She was named Marie, but was more often affectionately called Mimi. She grew up as "the little one" in a houseful of children that all seemed to be a lot older than she. Perhaps that was because, to them, she was always considered "the baby."

But I was loved and I knew it. When an earthly father is so full of love, how can one fail to understand the love of a Heavenly Father? When brothers and sisters tenderly support and shield, why would it not be easy to expect the same from Jesus who said, "Whoever does the will of my Father in heaven is my . . . sister" (Matthew 12:50)?

Mom and Dad, so recently immigrated to Canada, continued to speak low German at home. But at church, the services were in high German and my playmate across the lane also spoke high German. My parents also thought and acted and even ate in a way slightly different from their Canadian neighbors. Although these customs were sometimes an embarrassment in my growing up years, I later came to appreciate the contribution my cross-cultural upbringing made to my missionary career.

I was just a vulnerable 12-year-old when my family moved to British Columbia, about 1,500 miles to the west. The security of my sheltered childhood no longer supported me. The church we attended in the new hometown did not meet my spiritual needs and as a young teenager my relationship to Christ became less and less important.

But God was in control.

One day a friend introduced me to The Christian and Missionary Alliance and from the very first visit I felt like I had come home. There was just one problem—the church was 10 miles away. How could I, just a young teen, possibly be part of a church so far away?

Sitting in the congregation one Sunday morning I spied a family I recognized from my town and soon I became a regular passenger on their weekly trek to church. I will never forget the feeling of anticipation as, dressed in my Sunday best, I eagerly watched from my bedroom window for their car to come. Going to the Alliance church was the most important event in my week.

Many years later with clarified hindsight I was able to see that even then God was positioning me for the accomplishment of His perfect will and the answer to my mother's secret prayer.

## 2

# Little House on the Prairie

In 1934 in the small town of Osler, Saskatchewan, a child could grow up enjoying all the delights of the great, spacious prairie. What could be more fun than scampering through the meadow, a bucket brimming with water in one hand and a strong stick in the other, anticipating the excitement of ridding Canada of a few more pesky gophers?

As the water gushed down the hole the gopher, much to the delight of the young hunters, would come out sputtering and when evening painted a glorious flaming prairie sunset the tired boys could wander home secure in the knowledge that a loving family would be there to shelter them.

Returning from the gopher hunt, Norm would swing open the screen door into the kitchen. Little sister Sophie was there as usual and as usual she was teased unmercifully until she threatened to tell Mama. Norm, the tormentor, would gobble up his supper of pan-fried potatoes and smoked farmer sausage. He had plans for the evening.

If he was lucky, big sister Caroline might be coaxed into reading a book. There was no television and even if there had been, there was no electricity to run it. Sitting with a book in the warm glow of the oil lamp and, through the wonders of imagination, joining the Sugar Creek Gang in their escapades was endlessly thrilling and built character besides.

Norm's mother Nettie rested in the bedroom during those days of Norm's childhood. Her chronic illness was a great concern to her husband Ben and he worried about the future of his little family.

There were other concerns, too. Money was scarce. Year after year the summer wind blew hot and dusty and crops refused to grow. Farmers turned from raising grain to raising cattle which they turned out into the fields to graze on the sparse vegetation.

Ben spent long days in his truck making the rounds of district farms, picking up cans of cream and delivering them to the city of Saskatoon. In the winter, when the wind changed to icy blasts that drifted the snow in mountainous waves across the country roads, Ben would spend even longer hours in the freezing air shoveling a path for his truck. Providing for the needs of a family in those days was no easy task.

Norm realized early that he was expected to join in that work. When his dad came home

tired and hungry he would say to his eight-
year-old boy, "Sonny, drive the truck over to
Grandpa's for me, will you?" And drive it
Sonny did.

Every day Norm and Caroline had to see to it
that the ravenous appetite of the cook stove
was satisfied. When their dad came home in the
evening he would be sure to check the big
woodbox to see if it had been filled.

In that charming prairie town it was possible
to raise your own livestock. One spring day
Norm's dad bought him a piglet. He energetically set about to fatten it up, dreaming of the
handsome profit he would gain for his efforts.

There were other ways to make money, too.
Norm sped from door to door selling greeting
cards and delivered the Saskatoon *Star Phoenix*.
Life, he was coming to realize, was made up of
both work and play.

Norm was only nine when he discovered
that life had a spiritual dimension as well. The
town of Osler had been touched by the Holy
Spirit through the preaching of a local pastor
and the effects reached to the children as well.

Walking home in the darkness one night,
under a sky that showered the earth with mete-
orites, Norm faced the frightening reality that
he was not ready to meet the Lord if He should
return that awesome night. So after the next
Bible club meeting both he and Sophie committed their lives to Christ.

Young as they were, the Ens' children begged

their dad to let them clean out an old wooden storage shed which became their clubhouse. Several cream cans were placed in strategic corners and supported rough planks forming crude pews. Each day after school about 15 neighbor kids gathered there, not to *play* church, but to have a real service.

One distributed the little red song books. Norm played his guitar and Caroline told the Bible story. Day after day the neighborhood children scampered home from school to gather in their makeshift sanctuary.

Unknown to them at the time Norm and his sisters would soon find it necessary to draw on the reality of what they believed. When Norm was 12 years old his mother died and for two years a pervasive loneliness engulfed the family. One day, however, it became apparent that their father had chosen a new wife for himself and a new mother for his children.

They were overjoyed. In jest they sometimes referred to her as "Aunt Jamama" for she was their Auntie Annie, younger sister of their mother. This godly woman took on the awesome task of mothering three lonely but lively teenagers.

Ben was proud of his only son Norman, now a handsome Christian young man. Ben had purchased a business—Ben Ens' General Store—and he dreamed of the day it would be "Ben and Son." But one day he had to lay all his cherished dreams on God's altar.

"Dad," announced Norman, "I think the Lord is calling me to go to Bible school."

Pride and disappointment vied for the upper hand in Ben's heart. In his youth he, too, had wanted to be a minister. The thought that the Lord was now calling his son to fulfill that long-ago dream finally banished the disappointment.

"I will support you all the way, Son," the older Ens promised.

In 1953, young Norman Ens enrolled at the Canadian Bible Institute (now called Canadian Bible College).

Meanwhile, out in British Columbia . . .

# 3

# *Made for Each Other*

Norm shared my belief that in answer to our parents' prayers God was at work from the beginning, forming us according to His design. Since it was in His plan for us to one day belong to each other we believe He shaped us with that thought in mind. Long before we met we were being made for each other.

Although we were born only 30 miles apart we did not meet until we were in Bible school. We might not have met then either had it not been for my roommate, Eileen.

In 1954 rules at the Canadian Bible Institute in Regina, Saskatchewan, were strict. Young men and young ladies did not socialize and neither did young men and young ladies have the right to choose with whom they would sit at meal times. Each table had a young lady and a young man who had been carefully chosen by the staff to act as host and hostess for that table. Every week a new seating plan was posted and students sat where and with whom they were told. Eileen was hostess at one such table. The host was Norman Ens.

And there was another rule. Every student was required to do a certain number of hours of work each week for the school. They called it "gratis." They said it kept education costs down.

My gratis during that first semester was waitressing. One day I brought a big bowl of delicious stew to Eileen and Norm's table. Like most young men, the host of this table was always hungry.

"Wow, look at that," he exclaimed, eyeing the big bowl of steaming stew.

"What? The stew or the waitress?" giggled Eileen.

Glancing up into my face, Norm murmured, "The waitress!"

My brown eyes met his twinkling blues and that was the beginning. At first we thought we were just teasing each other, but soon we knew we were in love.

But those rules! As a first-year student Norm was allowed only a very brief "social privilege." Since I was a third-year student I got a bit more. We were able to split the difference.

Besides that precious time together once a week we were not to talk to each other except for the much-anticipated "15 minutes." Each day before supper couples were allowed to spend 15 minutes talking together in the chapel. All the couples—in the same chapel! The lights were turned down low and everyone tried to find a secluded spot. The young ladies arrived

as prettied up as possible, making liberal use of
the choicest, most fragrant hand lotion. The
young men appreciated that lingering fragrance!

No engagement could be formalized during
the school year. That was another rule! But
immediately after the commencement service
Norm and I drove to the park by the parlia-
ment buildings and Norm gave me a beautiful
ring.

How we thanked God for leading us to each
other. Psalm 48:14 became our life verse: "For
this God is our God for ever and ever; he will
be our guide even to the end." We were committed to each other and to our united future as
missionaries—somewhere, anywhere in the
world.

A few months later, at our wedding, the
soloist sang:

> *Let them burn out for Thee, dear Lord,*
> *Burn and wear out for Thee.*
> *Don't let them rust or their lives be*
> *A failure, my God to Thee.*
> *Use them and all they have, dear Lord,*
> *And get them so close to Thee*
> *That they feel the throb*
> *Of the great heart of God*
> *And their lives burn out for Thee.*

Those words expressed our intense and mutual desire to be used of God. His call on our lives
together was strong and sure. He would be
faithful—even to the end.

# 4

# *Pastor Norman Ens*

Norm was 23 and recently graduated from Bible school when he became a pastor. We had been married just one year and little David was only weeks old.

The Prairie Gospel Tabernacle of Heart's Hill, Saskatchewan, invited him to preach for a call. I still remember the day. We parked our green, 1950 Pontiac in the windswept parking lot of the church and surveyed the wide open spaces that surrounded the place.

Across the gravel road Farmer Craik's white-faced cattle gazed placidly back at us. Except for the owners of the cars parked beside ours not a soul could be seen. The landscape was dusted with snow and I hugged Davey to me as we entered the warm atmosphere of this humble house of God.

The friendliness of the congregation soon put us at ease and we joyfully joined them in the singing. As Norm rose to preach his painstakingly prepared sermon my heart rose up in prayer for him. Already we yearned to remain in this pleasant place with its good-natured people.

After the benediction had been pronounced Norm and I retreated to the basement apartment below the white frame church and nervously awaited the board's decision. Would Norm become the pastor of the Prairie Gospel Tabernacle or did God have some other place of ministry for us?

Soon we heard the board members descending the narrow stairs. With beaming faces they announced that by unanimous decision they were inviting Norm to be their pastor. God had answered our prayer!

After a delicious dinner, Norm and I headed back home to share the good news with his parents. It did not take us long the next day to load up our few possessions and by the following Sunday we were happily situated in our new basement home.

Unquestionably, life in Heart's Hill was considerably different from city life. But our response to any and all inconveniences was, "It's good missionary training!"

Our nearest neighbor lived more than a mile away and the nearest grocery store was three miles away. Power lines had not yet been strung to that part of the province so a generator in the garage noisily provided us with electricity. An oil heater in the middle of the kitchen-living room kept the apartment warm. Cooking was done on a coal and wood stove which also helped keep us snug during the blustery Saskatchewan winters.

There was no running water. We pumped our water from a well out in the yard. It was wet, but it was also rusty. When it was heated in a boiler on top of the stove the rust rose to the surface in a murky scum.

It was not the best for washing clothes so in the winter Norm waded out into the snow drifts and filled up the boiler. Melted on the coal stove, the snow provided nice clean soft water for washing Davey's diapers. In the summer months, however, our laundry took on a decided reddish tone!

Baths were taken with water heated on the stove and poured into the big galvanized tub in the kitchen, the warmest room in the house. One always hoped there would not be a knock at the door while bath time was in session!

When it snowed, drifts filled in the roads and church would be canceled. This gave us the pleasure of an enforced annual winter vacation.

Norm's salary, taken out of the weekly church offerings, was $25. One winter he set aside all the change from his pay and by spring had saved enough to buy a new suit. Besides the offering, Norm earned a little extra helping area farmers with the harvest.

And there was also an occasional gift of money, farm produce and an abundance of heavy cream in quart-sized canning jars. Puffed wheat with cream and sugar became our favorite nighttime snack. Norm gained so much weight that the doctor would not give him medical clearance to go overseas until he slimmed down!

And the congregation? It would be impossible to find a group of people anywhere more friendly or caring or appreciative than the people of the Prairie Gospel Tabernacle. In winter, when their work load was light, we spent countless happy hours visiting in their homes. Without exception they showered us with love and respect and, when Baby Shelly arrived to join our family, their delight was genuine and their gifts generous.

In that loving atmosphere during those three years at Hearts Hill we grew together in our relationship to Jesus Christ, learning more perfectly how to love and obey Him. It was a training custom-designed by our loving Heavenly Father for the next step in our dream—a dream that fast became a nightmare.

>-+-<>-O-<>-+-<

My mother's secret prayer—"Make this child your servant"—came to pass. Cambodia became our new home and her gentle people entwined themselves around our hearts. But Vietnam, Cambodia's neighbor, was at war and the conflict was spreading across the border. Anti-American sentiment skyrocketed as radios blared the raucous voice of Cambodia's Prince Norodom Sihanouk spewing forth indignities about the West.

Cambodia had never been truly open to the gospel but now, under such pressure-cooker circumstances, it became even more difficult to present the Christian message—"a western religion," they called it.

Emotionally it was difficult to be the objects of contempt. One day an incident took place that brought our missionary service in Kompong Speu to an abrupt halt.

A Cambodian village on the border of Vietnam was bombed by American planes. Women, some of them pregnant, and children had been killed. Posters denouncing this action immediately appeared in post offices and other public places. And once again Prince Sihanouk's voice raged over the radio, decrying the slaughter and promising revenge.

Our Mission chairman, Harry Taylor, fearing especially for the safety of the missionary women who were expecting babies (I was eight months pregnant), urged us to leave as soon as possible. Our hearts were sick. It had all been so exciting and now, so soon, it was over.

My eyes glazed with tears as I faced the sea of little brown faces in my children's class and listened to them sing songs that had previously brought me so much joy. *What will happen now to those precious people who have just begun to trust Jesus?* I wondered to myself.

And so we prepared to evacuate.

News that the "foreigners" were selling their household effects spread quickly and soon

droves of people were swarming into our yard
ready to buy up anything and everything. The
crowd became so large, the situation so serious,
that we locked our doors and began selling
things through the barred windows. Our wedding gifts, the children's toys, linens, kitchen
supplies—all were disposed of.

The last thing to go was our cherished pale
blue Volkswagen which had been purchased
with great delight just a few months earlier.
The Volkswagen's last task had been to carry
our family to the guest home in Phnom Penh
where we would await our flight to the relative
safety of Bangkok, Thailand.

Just four hours before the flight the
Volkswagen's new owner arrived. Norm sadly
watched him drive away with his treasure, then
quietly crept upstairs to join his sleeping family for a few hours of desperately needed rest.

Disillusionment mingled with relief flooded
into our hearts as we finally boarded the plane.
The dream, it seemed, was just that—a dream.
What the future held we did not know. Perhaps,
at that point, it was a blessing.

We finally arrived in Bangkok and our family
of five crowded into one little room at the
Mission guest house to await the determination
of our destiny. The only sure thing at that
moment was the imminent birth of baby number four. We settled in to pray and to wait.

Within days the instructions came: "Go back
to Cambodia!"

What? Go back to the country we had just left? Go back after we had sold all our earthly belongings and tearfully cut the emotional ties that were still developing? Go back to what? Missionaries usually go to the field with an adequate outfit. No one just "goes." But our outfit was gone. How would we live? Question after question streaked unbidden through our hearts and minds.

We struggled with the decision. *Would* we obey? How *could* we obey?

As one day flowed into another we began to think that perhaps it was possible. We could "rough it" if we had to—sleep on a kapok mattress instead of the comfortable North American bed we had sold; buy a daily chunk of ice to cool our food in place of using the refrigerator that now stood in someone else's kitchen; make do with what food we could buy locally. So what if our home lacked the embellishments of pictures and knickknacks? So what if we lived the remaining months or years of our term in poverty?

We decided to obey the directives of those in authority over us to go back to Cambodia, but we still had to await the birth of Rodney Benjamin.

The first time I held him my heart went out to him in pity. How I wished we could have had a pretty room all outfitted especially for him. He didn't even have his own bed! Of course, it was not he who minded. All he demanded was the loving care of his parents and of that he was assured.

The Mission suggested we stay in Bangkok until the baby was six weeks old. Those six weeks were a blessing in disguise for they gave us time to prepare mentally and emotionally for whatever lay ahead—at that point an unknown quantity.

Finally back in Phnom Penh we set about to establish a home once again. We heard that some months before, when American aid workers were evacuated, their furniture was placed in storage in a huge warehouse. The good news was that we could purchase whatever we needed.

Soon our little rented house was filled with North American beds, dressers, rattan easy-chairs, a stove and a kerosene fridge. In addition, many years earlier, a missionary had gone home sick. We were given access to her barrels filled with numerous small household items.

The truth was that in many ways we were better equipped than we had been in Kompong Speu. God, ever faithful, ever there, was showing us that He would never fail.

In the months that followed, with the war continuing to rage on the border with Vietnam, making a move back to the country unsafe, the Mission asked if we would be willing in our next term to go to Thailand. Anxious that our missionary careers continue, we agreed.

A year and a half later our first term ended

with two young missionaries considerably richer in both experience and faith. Our dream had come true, but not quite like we had planned.

# 5

# *Blinded by Dark Spirits*

They looked like beautiful ornate birdhouses, these interesting little structures perched on pillars beside every Thai home. But in front of each house lay an offering of incense sticks or fruit. These were not birdhouses—they were the homes of the household spirit, the spirit who through fear held sway in the hearts and minds of all who lived there.

One of the teachers in the local high school which was across the street from our home in Buriram became ill. The help of the spirits was invoked to heal her. The other teachers promised that if she got well they would build the spirits a house on the school property.

She recovered and they kept their promise. What a house it was! While most spirit houses were similar to a fair-sized birdhouse, this one was the size of a child's playhouse. Even an adult could walk around in it. When it was completed a medium was summoned to invite the spirits to inhabit the house. Many people gathered to watch as she went through her incantation.

Norm, too, was there to observe the proceedings along with one of the teachers who had become our friend and often came to our home to practice her English.

"I suppose you think we are crazy," she said to Norm with obvious embarrassment.

"Oh, no," replied Norm. "I know the spirits have power but Jesus' power is greater."

The ceremony ended with no visible indication that the spirit had occupied the house.

But another ceremony in another place was not so nondescript. The setting was a large circular area surrounded by neighborhood homes. Large tables had been placed around the perimeter and covered with various offerings to the gods. Music blared from a public address system.

In the middle of the circle a young man was dancing, obviously in a trance. Bystanders said he was not even from one of the families who were sponsoring the ceremony. He was simply a neighbor, they said, who having leaned out his window to listen to the music, became "possessed" and began to dance.

In another corner of the yard a group of people were endeavoring to help an old woman become possessed by a spirit. She could then be a channel into the spirit world for her family. But the woman seemed to be having trouble becoming possessed.

Then, suddenly, as the music changed beat, she began to dance, evidence that she was now fully under the influence of the evil spirits. The onlookers smiled, not perceiving the source of these spirits nor the bondage to which they were subjecting themselves. They also had not heard and did not understand that Jesus had come to deliver them from their darkness.

Boonma was a spirit medium, a channeler for any who wanted to contact other-earthly beings.

One day, Boonma's daughter, Mia, gave her heart to Christ. So every week we went to have a Bible study at the little house where Mia lived with her mother. And each week as we sat on the floor around a tiny oil lamp we carefully explained the Scriptures, particularly what they said about demons.

Mia and her mother learned that the spirits they were contacting were really demons who hated human beings and had as their ultimate objective the destruction of human beings. But, we told them, Jesus' power was infinitely greater. He could deliver anyone—even Boonma—from fear and bondage.

One evening Boonma was ready for that deliverance and she prayed to give her heart and life to Christ. *Wouldn't it be nice*, we thought, *if God could allow Boonma some tangible evidence that something real had happened to her and that she was truly free.*

That night Boonma had a dream. In her dream she saw a seven-headed cobra—a spirit creature—slithering up the rail of the stairway into her house.

"Go away," Boonma commanded. "We aren't having anything to do with each other anymore."

In the past it was she who had obeyed the spirits, but now she was commanding the spirit. It meekly turned and slithered back down the railing and out of her life.

In the same dream she saw an ugly, black, shapeless form rise out of the ground in the yard. Again she ordered it to leave and it, too, obeyed her. Boonma was encouraged to believe that she was delivered, completely free in Christ.

In a second dream, Boonma saw herself being chased by a whole crowd of angry spirits. Terrified, she searched in vain for a hiding place. Suddenly, a great hand reached down from above and scooped her up out of the malevolent reach of the demons. Boonma was gloriously free!

>─┼─◆─○─◆─┼─◄

One evening a well-groomed, handsome young man named Somchay came to our youth meeting. He seemed to enjoy the gathering and we invited him to come back. It was not long before he accepted the Lord and he began to pray with the group.

Then, early one evening just after dark, two of Somchay's friends arrived at our door.

"Please come," they begged. "Somchay is very sick."

We hopped on our motorcycle and followed the friends to the outskirts of town. The narrow streets were intimidating, the shadows forboding.

We finally pulled up in front of a dilapidated house and were ushered up a ladder to a darkened room. A young man stood before us naked from the waist up, his long black hair disheveled. *This could not possibly be Somchay*, I thought to myself.

Someone was trying to help him put on a pair of trousers but he could not seem to get his legs in the right places. We had thought we were coming to pray for someone who was sick with malaria or possibly the flu. How wrong we were!

My heart pounded with fear as the reality of his problem sunk in—Somchay was under the control of evil spirits. The atmosphere did nothing to assuage my alarm. In the dim light of the oil lamps an elderly man sat on the floor cutting noodles with a huge knife. *What if Somchay gets a notion to grab that knife*, I thought to myself, another stab of fear piercing my heart.

*No*, I decided firmly, *I will not be afraid of the devil.*

Norm and I stayed a while. We prayed. We explained what we thought was wrong with Somchay and we promised to return the next day with other Christians to pray some more.

The following day, along with three others, we once again gathered at Somchay's shack. We sang about the blood of Jesus. Somchay joined in, a silly grin often crossing his face. We talked to him. He acted as if he did not know what we were saying. But when we told him he was having trouble with demons he vehemently denied it.

We prayed and we urged Somchay to pray. But this young man, whom we had heard pray so well in our youth meetings, now asked, "What shall I read?"

Finally Norm said to him, "Pray after me."

"All right," Somchay responded meekly.

"Oh, Lord, I want to get better," Norm prayed with child-like simplicity.

"Oh, Lord, I don't want to get better," a voice from Somchay's lips sneered.

Some time later, when all our efforts seemed fruitless, we decided to leave. On the way home we recalled what Jesus said, "These kind do not come out but by prayer and fasting." So we set ourselves to fast and pray for Somchay.

On Sunday the group from the church returned to visit Somchay. Much to our surprise we found him normal and he readily acknowledged that he had had trouble with demons. But now he seemed to be free and we rejoiced in his deliverance.

How we wish that was the end of the story!

We later learned that Somchay's girlfriend, with whom he was living, was a prostitute. She was unwilling to leave her profession, not because she liked it, but because a poor country girl like her could never earn an equal wage in any other way. Neither was Somchay willing to break up with her.

We had to leave them at this impasse, still under Satan's bondage. Predictably, we later heard that Somchay's trouble with the spirits continued.

Although some like Boonma were set free and delivered from the bondage of dark powers, thousands of others, like Somchay, remain to this day under the fear and domination of evil spirits.

Our message was one of freedom and liberty by the blood of Christ for any person willing to have their blinded eyes opened.

# 6

# God in the Wilderness

We had come to Buriram province—with 584,000 people—in August of 1967. After a strenuous year in Bangkok learning our second language in six years we were ready and anxious to begin reaching people for the Lord. But it was much more difficult than we had imagined.

Yes, we could gather together a delightful group of young people who responded to us and loved to play games, sing and participate in a meeting. But few made a firm commitment to follow the Lord.

Yes, we could call the adorable local children to come to Sunday school and VBS and see them learn songs and Bible stories, but their parents remained firmly Buddhist.

One day Norm sat with a man and explained the gospel to him. The man listened, seemingly enthralled by the wonderful story. When Norm finished he asked, "Do you have any questions?"

"Yes," the man replied, "do you eat rice in your country?" It seemed like the ears of the people could not hear, their eyes could not see and their minds could not comprehend our message.

We built an attractive bookroom-chapel and faithfully held meetings. But only a handful of people came. When we invited them they always wanted to know how many others were coming. They did not want to be the first. Oh, how hard and dry was the soil of the hearts of Buriram province. What a spiritual wilderness!

In such an atmosphere of rejection and frustration it was only natural to turn inward and what we saw there was not much different from the spiritual landscape around us. Our own hearts too were parched and barren and dry.

But we knew that a wilderness was one of God's favorite places to meet people. He had done it in the Bible. Moses, John the Baptist and Paul all met Him in the wilderness. God, we knew, was willing to satisfy even our own personal need for a deeper walk with Him.

We decided to meet with our friends Tom and Sandi Wisley, who lived just three hours away on the same train line, and their Dutch missionary neighbors, the Van der Weeles, to seek God together.

One night, with all the children safely in the care of their amah, the six of us retreated to an air-conditioned bedroom. In a tight circle of prayer we pled with the Lord for a new dimension in our walk with Him. We cried out for a conscious awareness of His presence. We yearned for Him to manifest Himself in tangible ways in our personal lives and ministry.

How frustrated and weary we were of striving
to do the right things and attempting to work
for God with so little communication from
Him and so little real communion with Him.
Sometimes it seemed that our great and awesome God was no different than the idols that
were worshiped around us—silent and remote.

Norm especially grew increasingly hungry
for an assurance of being filled with the Holy
Spirit. In desperation he began to spend whole
nights in prayer. Aware that sin separates God's
children from their heavenly Father and from
His blessing in their lives, he spent hours con-
fessing his sin and seeking cleansing and forgiveness.

Then, with seemingly no word from heaven,
he began to slide almost imperceptibly into the
trap of Satan, our spiritual enemy.

*There must still be more sin in my heart*, he reasoned as he pled with God to reveal it. Rather
than focusing on God's forgiveness and power
and ability to control our circumstances and
perform His will in and through us, Norm continued on and on in deep introspection, turning
his attention on himself and his unworthiness
before God. But the heavens seemed like brass,
his relationship to God at an impasse. Day by
day his doubt and uncertainty spiraled decep-
tively downward.

One day Norm sought out Theo Van der
Weele.

"Please pray for me, Theo," he pled. "I want the certainty of the fullness of the Holy Spirit but I just can't seem to find satisfaction."

In the midst of the prayer time that followed the Lord spoke the pivotal words that would transform Norm's life from that moment on: "My son, I want you to be a fountain of praise."

As Norm pondered the meaning of this word from the Lord he began to understand that he had truly received cleansing at the moment of repentance and that he must take the focus off himself and his unworthiness and turn his attention toward God.

In the days that followed he began to sing to the Lord in joyous worship and adoration. He read the Psalms, making the ancient phrases his own. Praise became the gateway of assurance that the cry of his heart had been answered. In this gracious, simple way God was explaining to Norm the deep truth of death to self (Romans chapters 6-8).

Fountains began to take on a special meaning for us—fountains weakly squirting out a few meager drops, fountains bursting forth in gushes, multiple fountains forming a sparkling orchestrated display. An experience some years later in Barcelona, Spain, became particularly significant.

We had been involved in the deliverance of a demonized woman and were physically and emotionally drained by the battle. But before leaving Barcelona we decided to take a tour of the city, a tour directed by the Lord Himself that became a spiritual highlight of our lives.

Spain is known for its fountains and at one never-to-be-forgotten spot we found ourselves watching the biggest, most awesome display of fountains we had ever seen. As triumphant orchestra music surrounded us with its majestic sounds, dozens of reflecting lights danced through the leaping spray—a veritable symphony of praise.

As we gazed at the spectacle before us our hearts responded in a release of overflowing worship and gratitude for the victory God had won. The tension and tiredness dissolved away.

God in the wilderness? Oh yes! We—and the once demonized woman—were living proof that God meets people in the wildernesses of life. None is too dark or barren for Him.

## 7

# Willing to Die

It was 1969. The headlines were incredible. Prince Norodom Sihanouk of neighboring Cambodia had been deposed in a coup and replaced by a government friendly to the West. But his ouster produced a tragic consequence: the Vietnam war spilled over into Cambodia and the new government gave the Vietnamese and American forces permission to pursue the communists as they crossed the border.

There was another consequence of the change of government—a consequence as magnificent as the other was devastating. The missionaries were also allowed to return along with the soldiers and the artillery. The rising pro-American sentiment made it easy to share the gospel. To a people bound by fear, the Christians brought hope through the love of Christ.

One morning the telephone rang in the kitchen of our furlough home in Saskatoon, Canada. Norm answered. The next few minutes were spent mostly listening.

"Do you know who that was?" he asked as he replaced the receiver.

"I think it was the Mission office in New

York asking us to go back to Cambodia," I answered.

It was indeed! Other missionaries, we were told, were already there. And now we were also being asked to return.

Our whole family was seized by excited anticipation. Norm and I walked around the house singing long-forgotten Cambodian choruses. The children joined in our enthusiasm. For Doug, it was returning to his birthplace.

But then, all of a sudden, reality set in. There was a war going on in Cambodia. If we went there we might be killed!

The more we thought about it the more Norm and I became convinced that if we consented to go we would indeed lose our lives. Hadn't the Lord just recently urged us to plan for the guardianship of our children and to make a legal will? Was that just coincidence or was it a part of His overall plan to care for our children?

*Yes*, we thought, *if we agree to go to Cambodia we will probably die there.*

We were in a quandary. If we obeyed, we were sure we would die. If we disobeyed we might as well forget about serving the Lord. We knew we could not serve Him in disobedience.

The annual Council of The Christian and Missionary Alliance was being held in Houston, Texas that year. It was a long drive for us and as each of those 2,000 miles rolled by our hearts became more and more troubled. It was time to count the cost.

After a week of business sessions and inspir-
ing preaching it was finally time for the Sunday
afternoon missionary rally, always a highlight of
Council. The theme that year? Alliance missionaries who had been martyred or died while
in missionary service. I sat on the platform
with the other missionaries and thought, *Soon
they will be able to add our names to the list.*

At the end of the service time was given for
prayer. With a great flood of tears Norm and I
submitted our futures to the Lord. I thought of
the most awful things that might happen to
us—like being imprisoned in a cockroach-infest-
ed jail and other equally or more distastful
possibilities—and I prayed, "Oh Lord, if that is
Your very best for us, I am telling You now
that I am willing."

When it was all over we were astonished at
the joy that engulfed our hearts. We might
have expected peace because we had surrendered our wills to His, but the joy surprised us.
We sang all the way home to Saskatchewan.

＞—◀▷—○—◁▶—▷—◀

Our flight schedule to Cambodia took us
through Bangkok. We were delighted to be able
to spend an evening in prayer with Tom and
Sandi Wisley, our dear missionary colleagues. As
we chatted in the air-conditioned guest room
before praying Tom commented that one thing
he would never be able to do was to give someone a personal prophecy, a "thus saith the

Lord" message from the Lord. We all agreed that that would be a difficult thing to do.

We began to pray and a few moments later Tom suddenly blurted out, "Oh, God, forgive me for not being willing to say what I know You want me to say—thus saith the Lord." He went on to give a prophecy which included the words, "The waters of death will not overflow you."

Even as those words escaped his lips I knew in my heart that this was an authentic message from God and I was overcome with gratitude and amazement at the kindness of the Lord. On the eve of our departure to what we expected to be certain death God had given us the wonderful assurance of life.

The Lord, we came to understand, had not intended us to die—He only wanted us to be free from the crippling fear that hinders perfect obedience.

# 8

# *Signs of His Presence*

We arrived in Cambodia with a special and abiding sense of God's presence such as we had not known before. Sometimes He made us aware of His presence in humorous ways, as if He was sharing a joke with us.

Across the Mekong River in Phnom Penh was a settlement of refugees, some of whom were Christians from Vietnam. It was a special joy to worship with them and to see the fruit of the labors of our missionaries in that war-plagued country.

The refugees were very poor and in need of clothing, so the women of the Cambodian church, though themselves in need, remade used clothing for them. They often sat on my floor and stitched or used my electric sewing machine and my imported thread that I had brought from Canada.

Ah yes—the thread. I remember thinking to myself, *There goes my good thread. Now when I need some I will have to use the cheap, local thread that breaks so easily and is not colorfast.* I did not dwell long on this selfish thought but I have to admit that it crossed my mind.

It was my habit several times a week to summon a man pedaling a cycle to take me to a local Cambodian church where I taught an English class. At Christmastime one of my students handed me a beautifully wrapped package. I was touched by her kindness and placed the gift with others under our tree to be opened Christmas morning.

When the day arrived and I finally tore off the paper I found a lovely, flat, square box. Lifting the lid, I burst out laughing. The box was filled with little spools of thread in a rainbow of colors. It was not the easily broken, non-colorfast, local thread, but beautiful spools imported from France—a sign of His presence.

>─┤─◄►─�‒O‒◄►─┤─◄

One evening as we prepared for bed I commented to Norm, "Do you know what I am hungry for? Canned peaches or pears!" With so many kinds of delicious tropical fruit available it surely was a selfish whim to want something more besides, and canned at that!

The next day when I returned from teaching my English class I discovered a cardboard box sitting on the foot of the bed. Someone from World Vision had left some goodies. You can probably already guess what was in that box among all those things from "home"—a huge tin of pears *and* a huge tin of peaches!

We did not need the fruit as much as we needed to hear the Lord saying to us, *I am*

*right here with you every moment of the day and
night. I hear all you say even in the privacy of your
bedroom. I am looking after you.* Another sign of
His presence.

>-+<>-O-<>+-<

God even used the postal system to deliver
His special word of comfort and encouragement.

One day a beautiful postcard arrived from a
Catholic nun whom we had met in Bangkok.
The picture said it all. A tender hand was out-
stretched, the fingers curved gently upward. In
the hollow of the hand sat a tiny, fragile chick
crouched in absolute fearlessness, its wee feet
tucked under its delicate body. Clear, bright
eyes gazed out unconcernedly. And under-
neath, the caption read, "Be not afraid! Only
believe! Your Father cares for you!"

But that was not all.

Within days an identical message arrived
from a young Cambodian who was studying in
Paris, France. His postcard read, "Be not afraid.
You are in God's hand," another confirming
communication from the Lord assuring His
trusting children of His tender care for them. A
sign of His presence.

>-+<>-O-<>+-<

As the war raged on everyone around us
became poorer and poorer. The Cambodian
currency (riel) was quickly losing value. It took
a flight bag to hold it all when we cashed our

allowance check at the bank. As missionaries our financial needs were being met, but this was not always the case for some of our Cambodian brothers and sisters. We needed to learn about sharing.

Pastor Nil and his wife were lacking many things. One evening after a visit with them I gave Pastor Nil's wife a bottle of dish washing liquid. World Vision had given us a large container and it seemed to me we had enough and to spare. But soon my own container was virtually drained dry.

Pastor and Mrs. Nil came for another visit. As they left Mrs. Nil shyly asked, "Could I have a bit more of that soap?" I suspected she was using it for everything including laundry. In my mind it was too precious to be used for that and I did not want to share any more.

"They have more at the Mission guest house," I finally said, surrendering to my selfish instincts. "Go ask them and if they won't give it to you come back and I will give you some."

I could tell by the look on her face that if I wouldn't help her she would not have the courage to ask someone else.

*Too bad for you, then,* I thought to myself.

The next morning I knelt down by my bed and started to read my Bible where I had left off the previous day. Imagine my chagrin when I read: "Do not withold good from those who deserve it, when it is in your power to act. Do not say to your neighbor, 'Come back later;

I'll give it tomorrow'—when you now have it with you" (Proverbs 3:27-28).

I got up from my knees, went to the kitchen, poured out a little bottle of soap and sent it to Nil's wife accompanied by an explanation and an apology.

With the poverty of war and refugees on every side, God was giving us personal signs of His presence in special everyday kinds of ways. And I was learning, at times somewhat painfully, that we could be transmitters of those same signs of love to others.

# 9

# *I Believe*

It is a unique experience to care for children in a country that is at war. We always looked forward to having our four children home from Dalat School in Penang, Malaysia, for their vacation. But we also realized we were bringing them to a place of danger. We wanted them home to share in our ministry but we did not want them overcome by fear. And, most of all, we wanted to see them committed to doing God's will regardless of the cost.

Ever since the children were little we sang together as a family. As they grew up and learned to sing in harmony the songs became more and more interesting. Each vacation we would add a few more to our repertoire. One of the new songs in 1975 was *Why Should I Worry or Fret?*

> *I believe,*
> *I believe,*
> *I believe so why should I worry or fret?*
> *He holds the future in the palm of His*
> *    hand*
> *And He has never failed me yet,*

*I know He is reigning and still has control,*
*So why should I worry or fret?*

*There are some people who live each day*
*    in fear*
*Of what tomorrow will bring;*
*But I'm trusting in One who is walking*
*    so near,*
*I'm talking about the King of kings.*

*He told me He'd protect me and go with*
*    me each day*
*And, brother, I've no reason to doubt;*
*He's been so near me every step of the*
*    way*
*And He will surely lead His children*
*    out.*

Each day held potential danger but we had
decided to entrust our lives into the Lord's
hands and to go about our ministry confident
of His care. We also prayed about knowing
when we should withdraw if and when it
became necessary and that we would clearly
know and understand His will and timing.

We were not always without fear but, on the
other hand, it was exciting to know we were
being protected and led through a very difficult
time and place.

One day the Lord showed us the extent of His protection for our family in a very dramatic way.

Our house help were taking their usual siesta one warm, lazy afternoon. Norm was sitting at his big wooden desk in the little building behind the house conferring about literature with his Cambodian counterpart. The children were home from school and Doug and Rod were about to go to a nearby market.

A seemingly insignificant little argument arose between the boys about whether they would walk or ride their bikes and it delayed them a few minutes.

Dave had responded affirmatively to my request to be taken on the back of his motorcycle to the beauty parlor. We too were delayed just a few minutes as I made a quick check on the yeast rolls rising in the kitchen.

Before any of us could leave the house we heard a thunderous explosion. We ran toward the street and opened one of the two large metal doors that formed the gateway to our yard. As we stood in the opening, gazing out across the marketplace, several Cambodians joined us, scaling the wall to get a better view from the top.

Suddenly, without warning, the air was torn apart by another deafening blast that sent us dashing for the shelter of the house. As we bolted across the yard we were showered with flying branches from some coconut trees and other assorted debris.

The source of the explosion we found out was a rocket that had been dispatched by the Khmer Rouge from the outskirts of the city. It had come crashing in just 15 meters (about 50 feet) from our gate.

Several people instantly lost their lives. One man riding a bicycle was struck by shrapnel and came crawling to lean against our wall. A huge pool of blood gathered under the wounded limb as he waited there for someone to take him to the hospital. A window in our house was broken and the walls were pocked by flying metal.

Norm and I and the children stood in the shelter of the house and clung to each other, intensely grateful to the Lord that His protective hand had covered us.

When our nerves settled down we ventured back outside to join the crowds of people who had congregated to survey the damage. Seeing the pool of blood by the gate, I told Doug and Rod to get some water from the nearby tap and try to rinse it away. Doug grabbed the yard broom and Rod poured the water as they cleaned up the mess. As I watched them I was suddenly overcome with emotion to see my little boys—then just 9 and 11—cleaning up the horrible results of war.

That evening it was Doug's turn to lead family devotions. He found the perfect Scripture for us to read together and as his dad read it aloud, Doug kept nudging me with his elbow.

"He who dwells in the shelter of the Most High will rest in the shadow of the Almighty." (Nudge, nudge.) "You will not fear . . . the arrow that flies by day." (Nudge, nudge.) "A thousand may fall at your side, ten thousand at your right hand, but it will not come near you." (Nudge, nudge.) "For he will command his angels concerning you to guard you in all your ways." (Nudge, nudge.) "I will be with him in trouble, I will deliver him" (excerpts from Psalm 91). (Nudge, nudge.)

We were intoxicated with the joy of knowing that nothing could hurt us unless it was in the perfect will of our Lord Jesus who loved us.

The following Sunday we stood before the congregation at the International Church and joyfully flung the words from our hearts: "I believe! I believe! I believe! So why should I worry or fret?"

## 10

# A Very Special Doll

It was Christmastime. The children were coming home from MK school after four long months of separation. Our desire to help fulfill their Christmas wishes was only multiplied by the time and distance that separated us most of the year. We particularly wanted to grant Shelly her Christmas wish—a doll.

But it was not just any doll. Another little girl at school already had the kind she wanted. The doll was soft and cuddly and dressed in red flannel pajamas. Her brown hair was caught up in a cute little pony tail and, best of all, she came equipped with a ring attached to a cord. When the cord was pulled the doll whispered special little messages. Her name was Baby Secret.

We knew there would not be time to order anything from Canada, but Bangkok had lots of stores and we could probably find the doll there. The question was not finding it, but affording it once we found it. Dolls imported from the United States were priced far too high for a missionary budget. Sadly we decided that Shelly would have to be content with some other gift, that is, until we met Janet Taylor whose little girl Karen had a Baby Secret.

I could hardly believe my ears as Janet told me the following story.

On the Taylors' trip from America to Thailand the cord on Karen's doll had pulled out. Since the warranty was still in place, Janet wrote the company and asked them to replace the doll.

Time passed. No doll arrived. So she wrote a second letter. Some months later the doll finally arrived in the mail. Then another doll arrived, apparently in response to Janet's second letter.

"You can have the second doll for Shelly," Janet exclaimed. "There is a price on the box which we should send them. It isn't very much."

Shelly's eyes literally danced on Christmas morning as she hugged and cuddled the "miracle" doll. And what's more, our whole family received the gift of a special demonstration of the loving care of a heavenly Father who delights to see His children—and most especially His little children—happy.

&gt;—+—&lt;&gt;—0—&lt;&gt;—+—&lt;

Again and again God evidenced His care for our family in a myriad of ways not only physically but spiritually as well. We rejoiced as one by one our children accepted Christ as their personal Savior.

Roddy was just five when suddenly one morn-

ing he blurted out, "I want to give my heart to
Jesus, but I don't know how." Norm took him
to the bedroom where he explained how even a
little boy could pray and invite Jesus to wash
away his sins and come into his heart.

A few moments later I walked into the room
to find Roddy with a big smile across his face
and Norm standing beside him crying tears of
joy. I scooped Roddy up in my arms and as I
hugged him he spontaneously burst into song:

> *Prah Jesu chanuk,*
> *Prah Jesu chanuk,*
> *Prah Jesu chanuk Phayman.*
> Jesus wins the victory,
> Jesus wins the victory,
> Jesus wins the victory over the devil.

Can a little boy of five understand spiritual
battles? Absolutely! A victory over the devil
had been won that morning as a five-year-old
boy passed from the kingdom of Satan to the
kingdom of God.

But it was not long until Rod would experience firsthand that Jesus could win the victory
over the devil. His joyful song was no guarantee
that Rod would never again fear the enemy. On
the contrary, traumatic daily happenings during
the war in Cambodia began to cause him to be
unusually fearful. Dark places, dark shadows
and being alone all filled him with dread.

One day Shelly took Rod under her wing.

"Jesus is with you, Rod," she assured him in a sisterly fashion. Gesturing with her hands as one would clear a pathway through a crowd, she continued, "And wherever you go, Jesus says, 'Get out of here, demons. Get out of here, demons.' "

From that time on Rod began to understand who it was that was stronger and the cloud of fear lifted.

Roddy had a special gift from the Lord—the gift of empathy. He often identified with hurting people, a characteristic that became particularly evident one evening at a servicemen's meeting.

The Vietnam war was raging on all sides and our family had been asked to sing at a Christian Servicemen's Center. After a delicious meal, as we waited for the program to begin, one friendly GI engaged the children in conversation. Seeking to amuse and interest them he launched into a graphic description of how he dropped bombs from his plane.

"For example," he explained, "if you were going to bomb a boat you would get the boat right in the center of the circle where the lines cross and then you would drop the bomb and make a perfect hit."

Five-year-old Roddy sat enthralled.

Then after a moment he asked, "What do the people in the boat think of that?"

His poignant question was the response of a compassion that had been placed in his heart

by a loving heavenly Father who cared for
him—even as He cares for all His little children.

## 11

# *Time to Report*

The danger and uncertainty of wartime pried open hearts that had long been tightly locked against the entrance of the light of God's Word.

Cambodians were now coming by the hundreds to hear the gospel and to embrace the truth. The gospel had been preached in Cambodia for 50 years yet in 1970 only 600 people in a population of six million called themselves Christians. Now, in 1974, the number of believers was growing so fast that our Mission as well as others was finding it difficult to keep accurate records.

It was decided that the missionary corp needed more mutual collaboration and encouragement, so every Wednesday at 4:30 missionaries from the Alliance and the Overseas Missionary Fellowship gathered at our headquarters building.

These sessions proved to be most stimulating. We found out that groups of believers were springing up everywhere and the gospel was being preached where it had not been before, often with astonishing results. One Cambodian pastor reported a spontaneous working of God in which 1,400 came to Christ. Evangelist Ravi Zacharias preached a five-week crusade and 660 more believers were added to the church. Soon the number of churches in the city of Phnom Penh alone had risen to 15.

Of course, there were no church buildings. Often the house of God was the space between the pillars under a Cambodian home. Norm preached one Sunday to a throng of men, women and children crowded into one such open air sanctuary. At the end of the message 80 people eagerly prayed to receive the Lord.

Another man had an old river barge that had been beached. It became a church—appropriately named Noah's Ark Church. No chairs or benches filled this sanctuary. People sat on the floor as they habitually did in their homes.

Where there was a group of adults meeting there was also a children's class. Week by week I met with Dally, a young Cambodian woman, to translate Sunday school lessons and duplicate pictures on the Mission press. These were given to the teachers at a group meeting each Sunday morning. Someone would demonstrate the story and then the teachers would take the pictures home to color in preparation for their classes that afternoon.

Although the training and preparation of materials was very primitive, it certainly did not dampen the enthusiasm of the children who crowded into the meetings. Sarong-clad big sisters carried younger siblings on their hips. Barefoot, shirtless boys—big and little—left their play and joined in to sing lustily. The seeds of truth were being sown in the hearts and minds of thousands of Cambodia's children and teens.

Youth from the local churches took advantage of this spiritual thirst and sold literature along the river bank where people strolled.

One young passerby noticed an attractive little book called "Proverbs." Thinking it was a book of traditional Cambodian proverbs he purchased it. As he began to read he soon realized that what he had in his hand was not what he expected. His initial annoyance, however, soon gave way to enthusiasm for the wonderful words he was reading and he began to put them into practice.

Some weeks later he again strolled along the river. This time the Christian young people were being trained by Campus Crusade for Christ to witness using the Four Spiritual Laws. As someone shared the gospel with the young student he decided that, yes, he would pray to invite the Lord Jesus to be His Savior.

The Christians took the student to church with them. There, much to his surprise, he spied his favorite little book of proverbs among the other Christian literature for sale. Only then did he realize that it was God's Word to which his heart had responded.

Even Buddhist monks eagerly listened to the

gospel. Some were contacted through English classes offered by the missionaries. Coveted knowledge of the English language gave way to the more important knowledge of the Lord Jesus—who He is and why He came.

Although the war situation virtually imprisoned all missionaries within the confines of Phnom Penh, the gospel was reaching into the provinces through Bible correspondence courses.

World Vision, too, was extending the love of Christ to undernourished and orphaned babies in a bright, cheery center in one of the suburbs.

One day when we were visiting the center, nurses celebrated the birthday of the Cambodia director of World Vision, Carl Harris. Giggling with excitement, the nurses gently wrapped a special gift and presented it to him.

"Happy birthday, Carl!" they chimed in unison as they handed him the box. "Here is your gift. A lady in Toul Kok made it for you."

With a puzzled expression on his face Carl removed the colorful tissue and opened the box. There are no words to describe the emotions that flooded Carl's face and heart and the faces and hearts of all in the room that day, for there in the box was a tiny, premature baby boy! He had been left on the doorstep of the center by a poor Cambodian woman who had no resources to care for her infant son.

When all the missionaries had shared their

reports of God's working, we ate our sand-wiches and then joined in prayer for divine guidance and protection for us and for the emerging church in Cambodia.

Before the 9 o'clock curfew rolled around we all poured out into the dark streets joining fear-filled people hurrying to the shelter of their fragile homes. *Our* hearts, on the other hand, were secure in our loving Lord.

# 12

# *The Survivor*

"**L**ook at that plane!" cried Yos Oan from the back seat of our car. "I think it's going to crash."

He was right! Columns of black smoke rose ominously into the clear blue sky as the plane hit the ground and burst into a ball of flames.

Stepping on the accelerator, Norm turned toward Chomka Moan, a compound of wood and thatch dwellings for the families of men enlisted in the Cambodian army. A disgruntled soldier, we soon found out, had decided to drop his load of bombs on the presidential palace located next door to Chomka Moan. But he had miscalculated. Instead of destroying the palace, dozens of family dwellings sheltering helpless women and children were being devoured by the inferno.

We watched from the car in horror as people poured out onto the road screaming in terror. Behind them, billowing flames raced from home to home engulfing the entire community like kindling.

Then we saw Heng. She was stooped over in pain and shock, a dirty cotton sarong drawn tightly around her to conceal the terrible burns that covered her lower back and legs. She had been warming her baby's bath water at a little kerosene stove when the bombs fell. The explosion tipped over the stove drenching the floor with burning gas. Her skirt burst into flames and the baby rolled from her arms into the fire.

I jumped out of the car and ran to her.

"Get in the car," I urged. "We will take you to the hospital."

She crawled into the back seat on all fours, unable to sit down. Then we spied a sobbing, terrified, little girl with a screaming baby on her hip. The baby's face had been burned and her arm blackened. The skin was already beginning to blister. I urged them both into the car. We did not know that the woman already in the car was the mother of the children.

We drove as quickly as possible to the military hospital. Heng was admitted immediately but the attendants told us that they had no facilities for babies and directed us to the main hospital.

The confusion at the second hospital was indescribable. The fire victims now beginning to arrive only added to the already crowded conditions. All that was available for our little seven-month-old was an adult-sized single bed with bare springs. No mattress. Not even a sheet. No nursing care. It was expected that some family member would look after the baby.

The baby's big sister was only 10. How could

this already traumatized little girl care for a
badly burned baby in these circumstances?

"Come," I said to her softly, "You can stay at
our house."

So baby and big sister came home with us.
Our housemaid invited the girl to sleep in her
room and the baby stayed with Norm and me.

We took the baby to see Dr. Dean Kroh.
Dean and Esther were Alliance missionaries
who had come to work in the World Vision
hospital now under construction. In the meantime they were treating patients in makeshift
refugee centers around Phnom Penh.

Dean skillfully treated the tiny arm and hand.
The puffy little face had one eye squeezed shut
and we wondered if it would ever see again.

The baby was used to being nursed. Now
even this small comfort was denied her. Hungry
and in pain she screamed angrily as we tried to
feed her from a bottle. I wept as I gently rocked
her in the swing on our front porch feeling as if
I held in my arms all the suffering of this sad,
sorrowful city of Phnom Penh.

By and by the swelling in the little face went
down. The eyesight thankfully was not damaged
but the baby was left with a large lightly pig-
mented area covering most of one cheek. Her
arm was badly scarred and two fingers were
gone entirely.

Day after day we visited the mother in the
military hospital. Nursing care was nonexistent there, too. Heng's husband tried to help

but what did a soldier know about caring for a burn patient? Esther Kroh spent many hours tenderly bathing her and offering her love and encouragement.

Still, Heng's suffering was incredible. As we walked down the hall to her room we could smell the awful stench of her third-degree burns. Maggots crawled through the wound that covered her lower back and both legs. There was no possibility of skin grafts. It seemed impossible that she would ever recover.

However, one day several months after the bombing, Heng came hobbling through our gate. She looked like Cambodia's representative to the Olympic pole vaulting team as she sported a long pole to help her walk.

Grotesque scars now closed her wounds and thick, bumpy hide had replaced the soft tan-colored skin. But Heng had survived! She was alive! With great simplicity Norm explained the gospel to her and wondrously her spirit came alive as well. We rejoiced over this dear woman saved not only from the awful fire of Chomka Moan but from the eternal fires of everlasting pain and loss.

But the story isn't over. Seventeen years later, Norm revisited Phnom Penh. Early one morning he answered a knock at his hotel room door. When he opened it a Cambodian woman threw herself at his feet and clung to them. Norm looked questioningly at the friend accompanying the woman.

"It's the burned lady," she whispered.

Hundreds of thousands of people in those intervening years had lost their lives during the Cambodian holocaust but this brave woman had survived. It was a miracle!

Tears welled up in Norm's eyes.

# 13

## *The Most Difficult Thing*

Ask 100 missionaries who also happen to be parents, "What is the most difficult thing about being a missionary?", and probably the answer will be unanimous: "Sending children away to boarding school." Every other problem pales by comparison into paltry insignificance.

On the eve of those days of separation Norm and I would often kneel with our four children and cry and tell the Lord Jesus how very difficult it was. But we would also tell Him that He was worthy—yes, surely He was worthy—of absolutely anything He might ever ask of us. And together we would all determine to surrender our loneliness to Him.

But that determination was often tested. It was tested when I sat alone in the bright, sunny bedroom of the first-grade girls at Dalat School and looked at all those miniature dresses hanging in the closet. I felt like I was in Gethsemane as I contemplated leaving six-year-old Shelly there.

It was tested as we sent Doug to join his older sister and brother at Dalat. He had his sixth birthday party in Bangkok enroute to Penang, Malaysia. He seemed even more vulnerable with his eye still black and blue from a collision with the dining room table.

It was tested when David, in grade five, wrote a letter begging us to let him come home, offering heartrending but impractical suggestions about how we could manage his schooling some other way.

It was tested for our youngest, Rod, when he was in grade two and his older brothers told him he would be at boarding school all by himself one day because they would finish before him. It was no comfort to a seven-year-old to be assured that it would probably be okay because he would be a junior by that time!

The saddest days were when we took the children to the airport and said good-bye. Coming home to an empty house still strewn with reminders of the childrens' presence, we wanted only to go to sleep for a couple of hours and try to forget that it would be another four long months before we would see them again. Then I would furiously clean the house, trying to hide the poignant remembrances.

One lonely morning after watching the departure of the plane carrying its priceless cargo to Malaysia I knelt by the green wicker chair in our Phnom Penh living room.

"Oh Lord," I agonized, "please accept the sacrifice I am making for You in sending my precious children away again."

Gently I heard His voice to my heart.

"It isn't really like that, is it?" He seemed to ask. "It isn't that you have decided to make some kind of great offering and so you are sacrificing your children to Me. Isn't this rather just a part of what is required by your overall obedience to My will?"

"Well, yes," I agreed. "It's more like that."

I was overwhelmed by the next impression: "To obey is better than sacrifice."

The thought surprised me.

Rising from my knees, I went to the dining room to join Norm for breakfast. He opened the *Daily Bread* and read the verse for the day, "To obey is better than sacrifice" (1 Samuel 15:22, KJV).

This was surely far more than an incredible coincidence. As I reflected on what the Lord might be seeking to say to me I realized that He desired that our obedience should be willing and without a great display of reluctance and anguish. As a parent I appreciated my children's willing uncomplaining obedience. If a task was truly too difficult I wanted them to ask for my help and I would gladly give it. I knew that my loving heavenly Father was like that. To obey was better, but to obey willingly, joyously was best.

Some people wonder: what happens to the

relationship between a child and his parents when at the tender age of six the child is sent far away from home?

What happens when the child is not afforded the opportunity to share schoolday joys and troubles with his parents?

What happens when the parents seldom or never get to attend a special school concert or sports event?

What happens when Mom and Dad are not there to defend the child when he or she gets embroiled in conflicts?

What happens when someone else is making the birthday cakes and giving the goodnight kisses?

What happens when for four long months the only communication is a weekly letter?

Does that child become bitter against his missionary parents or worse yet against God? Or do the parents themselves become angry at God for demanding such a sacrifice?

These are troublesome questions that plague the minds of missionary parents and grandparents. It is then that obedience is tested.

We know from personal experience that when the decision to obey no matter what the personal cost may be has been firmly made that faith can then reach out and a parent can say to a little first-grader being left in a distant country: "Mommy and Daddy are not here with you but remember Jesus said He will never leave you. He will always be with you." Parent and child alike learn to abandon themselves and each other to this unfailing security.

I remember the happiest day of the year was when we threw ourselves into each other's arms at the airport welcoming our brood back home once again.

I remember the excited chatter as we brought the children into the house and shared thoughts and feelings and events in an atmosphere of love and concern for each other.

I remember staying up late and just talking, getting caught up on four months worth of news.

I remember the children accompanying us on missionary trips. Each trip and each song we sang together was savored because of its rarity.

I remember the children entertaining us and each other with skits that made tears of laughter course down our cheeks.

I remember the wonderful annual vacations at the beach in Thailand. Being there together as a family was what made it special.

I remember reading together. C.S. Lewis' charming books transported us to the land of Narnia as our children began to understand concepts of eternity.

I remember praying together. "Everybody pray for the person on your right," Norm would instruct us. They learned to share each other's hurts and hopes.

I remember singing together. We sang as we practiced to participate in the International

Church services. We sang as we worshiped the Lord together in family devotions and we sang as we walked along the roads together. When we weren't singing ourselves, the old reel-to-reel tape recorder filled our home with Christian music.

One day I quietly eavesdropped on three-year-old Doug as he sat on the cement just outside the window. His fat little legs were crossed in front of him and his blond head was bent intently over his toys, his baby voice offering a praise song of his own composition to the Lord. Music filled our home.

I remember cooking extra-special delicacies and feasting on them together. A bowl of jello made from a packet that had traveled halfway around the world from Canada was always an exciting treat.

I remember agonizing together when discipline was necessary because no one wanted anything to spoil the few precious weeks we had to enjoy one another's company.

I remember the pain and embarrassment of Shelly's comment after an argument between her parents: "Mommy, it seems like you don't love Daddy."

I remember that we loved and respected each other in a way that was extraordinary, the kind of love and respect that may be missing in homes where constant togetherness causes children and parents to fail to appreciate each other.

We did not easily separate ourselves from our children. We did not do it because we thought it would be better for our relationship if we were apart from each other. We did it because God asked us to. And God always blesses obedience.

One of the greatest blessings I have ever received was a Mother's Day letter written by Shelly. Shattered relationships with teenagers often drive parents to their knees in broken-hearted prayer. Mindful of this fact, I marvel at the treasure that 14-year-old Shelly sent me that day:

> *Dear Mom:*
>
> *I just wanted to write you this Mother's Day and tell you how much you mean to me. Lots of kids are writing home to their moms and telling her what she means to them.*
>
> *I'm sure that when us kids were born you asked God to help you to be a good mother and that we'd follow God. Mom, God answered that prayer. He's given you the patience you need with us when sometimes all we are is little brats. We're sorry for giving you the few hard times we've had, but when we come back to school we've always had wonderful memories of our time together.*
>
> *We'll never feel unwanted because there's always you and Dad to show us*

*the unending love we feel. I really thank the Lord for having you and Dad as parents and how He's made you trust Him for the little and big things in life.*

*It's helped us in our spiritual growth to see the close tie we have as a family and with God. I can trust Dad and you for all my problems and I feel free to share them with you knowing you'll always understand and have a precious little saying and help for me.*

*You never think I'm stupid for doing something or acting in a certain way. I love to see the wonderful way you care so much for people God's sent you to minister to and the way you show your testimony and the way it helps others.*

*You're so brave in trusting God to take care of all your needs. I can't overlook the talent God has given to you for cooking, sewing, understanding, godliness, love, kindness, trust, help and everything else a mother is supposed to be, but you do even extra little things and I wouldn't trade you for any other mother in the whole world.*

*I just want you to know I really appreciate and love you very much and thank God for you. I will always look upon you for an example for my life.*

*Love, Shelly*

Does obedience work? Yes, it works! When the motive for the separation is obedience, relationships between an MK and his or her parents can be good and strong and loving. Relationships between the MK and his or her Lord can be firm and comforting and lasting.

Shelly's walk with the Lord Jesus led her through the difficult adjustment from MK boarding school to a secular high school in Canada. The Lord arranged for her to be able to combine grades 11 and 12, evidence of the high standard of the Dalat School for Missionary Children.

He walked with her as she attended Canadian Bible College. He brought her to the husband He had chosen for her, Blaine Sylvester. He took them as missionaries to Côte d'Ivoire, Africa. He gave them Tyler, Kristie, Adam and James.

Inevitably, Shelly and Blaine will face the same question: "What happens to the relationship between a child and his or her parents when at the tender age of six the child is sent far away from home?"

## 14

# *The Crazy Lady*

She roamed the streets dressed in filthy garb, her face smudged, her hair matted, her mind and spirit as disheveled as her appearance.

Was she crazy?

Or drunk?

Probably both.

Who could know what suffering and heartbreak had brought her to this terrible state?

With compassion prompted by the sure knowledge that Jesus loves even such as these, we reached out to her. Often she would come to our door asking for a little rice or a coconut from the bountiful supply that the palm trees surrounding our house produced.

We offered her so little, yet she came to visit us often. There was a curious satisfaction in our hearts at being able to help ease her miserable life.

One day on impulse I leaned over and kissed her dirty cheek. She did not appear to take special notice. But on her next visit, as she again prepared to leave, she drew close and whispered, "Will you kiss me?"

Coming home on a cyclo one morning I noticed a crowd of people hanging over our fence. As I walked through the gate I saw the crazy lady at the water tap in the corner of our yard. It was not unusual for her to be there. Sometimes she caught rats and brought them to skin and wash and eat.

But as I approached I could see the thing in her hand was not a rat but a tiny baby! It was dead. The woman had been scavenging in the garbage cans at the market and had discovered it there.

Who had thrown away this precious newborn? Who was really crazy?

The fragile body was gently washed and wept over and we offered our demented friend a tiny plot in our back yard where she could bury it.

Another day, I was sauntering through the vegetable market, my wicker basket on my arm. Suddenly we met. Her greeting was warm and exuberant. As I walked away I overheard her tell a merchant, "That lady and I used to be in jail together!" I giggled to myself. And no doubt at that moment I, too, appeared a bit strange!

One evening she called me to the gate. Looking earnestly into my eyes she whispered in a conspiratorial voice, "Be careful! They are out to get you!" Though I was amused, I was also touched by her evident care and concern for me.

I still think about the crazy lady. Did she

understand enough of the message of Jesus that she could turn to Him and find eternal peace and love?

I wonder. Maybe someday . . .

# 15

# *Baboo*

The morning quiet was suddenly shattered by a huge blast. With Phnom Penh under siege we were getting somewhat accustomed to such sounds. Still, they always brought painful questions such as, "Who will have been hurt this time?" We certainly did not know in that moment that the answer to that question would change our lives forever.

A Khmer Rouge bomb had been secretly hidden in a push-cart full of fruit. The plan had been that the bomb would be propelled into the nearby army camp. But something had gone wrong. Instead of hitting the camp, the bomb merely shot across the road and exploded.

Mrs. Paw Yon had just been to visit her soldier husband stationed in the camp. She said good-bye and started off for home, her baby daughter in her arms. The child started to fuss so Paw Yon sat down on a box in the street and nursed her.

Then it happened. The force of the blast flung the baby out of her arms and Paw Yon was hit in the head with a fragment of shrapnel. Someone had taken her to the hospital, convinced that she would not live.

We were informed that a mother, sitting in the street nursing her baby, had been killed.

*If the nursing mother is dead the family will need baby formula*, I thought to myself. I knew that World Vision stocked formula so I set off to get some and to try to find out where the family lived.

"I heard that the mother of a baby was killed," I said at the door of one house.

"No," came the answer. "She did not die. She was badly injured but she is still alive. She is in the hospital."

With my little gift of powdered milk I made my way to the hospital. What a sight met my eyes! There lay the mother, her head swathed in bandages, her arms tied to the bed rails. And by her side stood the father holding in his arms a sobbing little girl about 10 months old. She wanted her mommy.

The father was beside himself not knowing what to do. Suddenly I realized that this family needed a lot more than a few cans of powdered milk and before I knew it I heard myself offering to take the baby home and care for her until the mother was well again.

And so it was that our house emptied of children when our own all left for boarding school again had a baby that we could love. We called her "Baby." One day she tried to repeat her name but all that came out was, "Baboo." So Baboo she became.

Baboo soon learned to walk. She also learned that if she reached up as high as she could at the piano she could make beautiful tinkling sounds. She looked darling in the little clothes I sewed for her. Our own children returned from school for Christmas break and were delighted with their pretend baby sister.

Finally Baboo's mother was released from the hospital and Baboo went back to live with her family. Paw Yon's injuries had indeed been severe leaving her with one arm virtually useless and one foot that dragged along limply. She knew she could never keep up to a toddler and their little shack was near the river. We found out later that in order to assure her safety Baboo had been obliged to spend her days on top of the big wooden bed in the house. At least her mother knew where she was.

One day Baboo arrived back at our door. What a shock! Instead of the beautiful, cheerful child we had said good-bye to some months earlier, she was a sick, tragic looking little girl.

We got medical help for her and found the family a more suitable place to live. We urged them to continue to bring Baboo to us if she ever got sick again and explained that it was essential to boil her drinking water to avoid recurring dysentery. The mother in turn explained to us that she was incapable of walking about to gather sticks to make a fire to do this.

One day the parents asked if we would consider adopting Baboo and raising her.

"She was really supposed to be yours," the mother said. "She got into the wrong reincarnation by mistake."

We loved Baboo very much but decided that instead of taking her away from her mother we would help raise her. We envisioned her growing into a beautiful teenager, having the advantages of a good education and perhaps learning to play the piano. And so it was that our house became Baboo's second home.

Once as I was typing a letter she crawled up and stood behind me on the chair. She was just tall enough to reach her arms around my neck from behind.

With her mouth next to my ear, she started to sing: "We ah one in da Spilit, we ah one in da Lah!" Yes! In English! How did she know that these strange sounds meant something to me, that the truth of what she was saying described the relationship that she and I enjoyed together? Yes, we did have a special relationship, our family and Baboo. Yes, we were one in the Spirit, one in the Lord.

Then came February 23, 1975. All missionaries were given four days to prepare for evacuation. We kissed our little Baboo good-bye, our hearts refusing to believe that we would not be able to return to her and to Cambodia. No one dreamed that soon most of the little ones like Baboo would be dead, victims of Pol Pot's terrible massacre.

Safely back in Canada we often had a few leftovers after a family meal. *Just enough for Baboo*, I inevitably thought.

One evening we gathered in the living room to pray. Shelly prayed particularly for Baboo.

"Maybe," she exclaimed, "Baboo is already with You and she has the beautiful home that we always wanted her to have."

My heart was saying, "Precious little one, one day we will hug you again in that most beautiful of all homes!"

# 16

# *Adieu*

We had hoped and prayed that it would not come, at least not yet. But the unwelcome yet inevitable telegram had arrived: "All missionaries in Cambodia are to leave the country within four days. This is not optional." It was signed by the president of The Christian and Missionary Alliance, Dr. Nathan Bailey.

Called to a special meeting at the Alliance headquarters, we missionaries sat slumped in our chairs, stunned and unable to hold back the tears. Our field director, Eugene Hall, shared a Scripture the Lord had given him: "We have received good at the hand of the Lord. Shall we not receive evil?" (paraphrase of Job 2:10).

In spite of the hardship and danger, it had been so good to be in Cambodia and to witness the remarkable growth of the church. It seemed unspeakably evil to have to leave our Christian brothers and sisters behind and consent to the dreadful possibility that their beautiful country was about to fall to the communists.

We wanted to refuse the order, to say, "No, we will not leave. We will stay. We will trust

God." But we knew we must obey those over us in the Lord. They no doubt had information not at our disposal.

And indeed they did. God had provided in the International Church in Bangkok two ranking Christian men in the American military. They knew that as far as the state department was concerned Cambodia was expected to fall into the hands of the communist Khmer Rouge in approximately 10 days.

With concern for the missionaries still ministering there unaware of the situation, these men had intercepted Dr. Bailey at the Bangkok airport during a brief stopover. If he wanted the missionaries out before the takeover came, they told him, he must order an immediate withdrawal. Dr. Bailey authorized them to send a telegram in his name without delay.

Our missionary corp had been praying in anticipation of this news. Our prayers had taken the form of a three-point outline: "Oh Lord, we beg of You to let us stay in Cambodia! You can keep us safe. We know it because You have done it in the past. But if we must leave, please let us all go together. When that day comes may we all have the same impression. And Lord, please let us know in time so we can leave in an orderly fashion. May we not have to run away in fear and confusion. Lord Jesus, we are concerned for our Cambodian brothers and sisters. When evacuation time comes, may they also perceive it. Let them agree with our decision to leave."

God graciously answered all three of these requests.

On Saturday, February 22, 1975, one of the church lay leaders strode into Norm's study. Without even raising his hands in the customary Cambodian greeting he blurted out, "Pastor, I came to tell you that you can leave if you want to. I won't hinder you anymore." (At that point no plans had yet been made to evacuate the missionaries.)

"Thank you," responded Norm, somewhat surprised, "but I am not planning to go anywhere."

"Well, I just wanted to let you know," countered Sin Suem. Point three of our prayer outline had been answered even before we knew the call to leave was imminent.

The reaction of the whole Cambodian church mirrored that of Sin Suem. Though their hearts were breaking they agreed that the missionaries should go.

The fateful telegram gave us permission to wait four days. We spent these precious hours bidding tearful farewells to our many friends and turning over the work to the national church.

There was also time for missionaries and church leaders to share a last meal. With heads bowed and hearts entwined the situation was committed to the Lord again and again in prayer.

For us personally evacuating meant that once again we were leaving behind all the things we had accummulated since the last time. From all our possessions we managed to choose just enough to fill a few suitcases. And in a shoulder bag Norm carried the most valued treasure of his young sons—their Lego blocks!

On Thursday, February 27, a plane provided by the American embassy taxied into position at the Phnom Penh airport and dozens of heavy hearted passengers, all missionaries of The Christian and Missionary Alliance and the Overseas Missionary Fellowship filed on board.

In Bangkok we received the news that Phnom Penh had surrendered. The report said that, as black-pajamed troops (Khmer Rouge) rode tanks into the city, swelling crowds of jubilant inhabitants cheered them on. Everyone was simply glad the war was finally over.

Naively they supposed that their former lifestyle would be restored. Neither they nor we were prepared for the unspeakable horrors that awaited our people—the gentle people of Cambodia.

Meanwhile we found ourselves once again at the Alliance guest house in Thailand. Only three-and-one-half short years earlier we had left it to enter Cambodia for the second time. Now we were at another crossroad in our journey. Where would our path lead this time?

## 17

# *Surrender*

On April 14, 1975, the early morning babble of voices inside the homes of Phnom Penh was suddenly interrupted by a strident message from loudspeakers mounted on army vehicles making their way slowly through the streets.

"Phnom Penh is in danger of being bombed by the Americans. The entire city is to be evacuated. Everyone will leave for a duration of four days. You will leave immediately. Do not lock your doors. Your possessions will be safeguarded."

Stunned into silence the people stared at each other, their eyes clouded with apprehension as the meaning of the announcement penetrated their understanding.

Within minutes the streets were crammed with dazed and frightened men, women and children. Older children carried young siblings on their hips while their mothers and fathers bore on their heads or in their arms the family's four day supply of rice and clothing.

A privileged few tied their cargo to bicycles or motorcycles and pushed them. Others, who boasted the advantage of a car, loaded it and, in the absence of gas, used manpower to inch it along the road amid a sea of pedestrians.

Families tried frantically to stay together as they were forced by soldiers to flow with the throng. Like the tributaries of a great and ominous river they shuffled through the streets leading to the highway out of the city.

Passing the hospital they were horrified to see gravely ill and wounded patients being carried or dragged away as the corridors were evacuated. A few foolishly brave individuals refused to comply. Shots rang out and their dead bodies became a mute warning that Khmer Rouge orders were not to be taken lightly.

Identical instructions were broadcast in Cambodia's second largest city, Battambang. And, in addition, soldiers who had served under the former government were urged to report with their weapons. They would be reregistered, the announcement said, in the new army.

Instead, now defenseless, having been relieved of their weapons, they were executed.

High-ranking officers were told to dress up for a special meeting with Prince Sihanouk. Transported into the country for the supposed rendezvous, they were instead gunned down in cold blood.

As night fell at the close of that first confusing day friends and relatives huddled together for comfort and a fitful rest. The following

morning they again took to the road. After
several days of walking, their strength dissipat-
ing with each step, the crowd was organized
into communes.

It soon began to dawn on the people that
there had been no threat of American bombers,
nor were their homes and possessions being
safeguarded for them, nor would they be
returning in four days.

Instead, this was the beginning of a lifestyle
that cannot be imagined, a lifestyle that many
refused to believe could possibly be true. Parents
and children were separated. Adolescents were
placed in separate communes. The youngest
children were looked after by the very old.
Everyone, including small children, was obliged
to go to work building dams or planting or
harvesting rice.

It was arduous work for educated city resi-
dents who had no experience in manual labor.
Perhaps they could have learned had it not
been for the fact that at the end of a strenuous
day they hungrily returned to their commune to
be served not a hearty meal of rice and meat,
but a thin rice gruel, the main meal of the
day.

Sickness was soon rampant. Medicine was
nonexistent. The death count mounted as starvation and disease took their ultimate toll.

It quickly became common knowledge that
anyone with more than a third grade education
was doomed to execution. Soon all doctors,

teachers, soldiers or anyone literate (wearing glasses) disappeared, victims of a nighttime summons. A quick, sharp whack with a hoe to the back of the neck ended their lives.

Family members stoicly internalized their grief, fearing that the next call would be for them. No criticism of the new regime was tolerated. A pathetic atmosphere of mistrust pervaded every settlement.

Frequently, when a rumor surfaced that someone was marked for execution, the supposed victim would make a frantic flight to freedom in Thailand. That choice was indeed costly. He must leave behind his wife and children knowing that the possibility of reunification was slim. He must face the sure knowledge that if caught he would be executed. He must brave the dangers of the forest that stood between him and safety in Thailand. He must traverse mine fields and avoid heartless Thai robbers. Yet the alternative—death—drove hundreds into camps just over the border.

Arriving there, many were convinced that if only they could tell the story of what was happening in their country help would be forthcoming. How disappointed they were to discover that this was not the case. Their loved ones were doomed to continue to suffer.

Uniformity of appearance was enforced. The beautiful long dark hair of the women and young girls was cropped. Everyone dressed only in black. Long, black sleeves hid lithe, tan-skinned arms as the girls were taught that it was a shame not to keep them covered.

From time to time marriages were organized for young men and women who were deemed of age. The communist authorities chose a young man's mate, placing her hand in his and pronouncing them married. In theory the girls had the liberty to refuse the man to whom they were given but not many dared object.

Hopelessness and hunger caused the most unimaginable atrocities to be committed. A young mother left her little girl with a babysitter. When she returned the child had disappeared, a tragic victim of the hunger that deranged the sitter, driving her to cannibalism.

Evenings were frequently occupied by indoctrination sessions. Weakened in body and broken in spirit, most people meekly received the instruction.

It seemed that Cambodia had fallen into a deep, dark well from which there could never be any hope of escape.

## 18

# "A Saint for Heaven"

Once again, with an uncertain future facing us, we sought the Lord about where He desired us to go, what he desired us to do. I counted the number of times we had pulled up stakes—20 moves in 20 years.

I recalled the special verse of assurance the Lord gave us one morning as we left one of our many homes: "Lord, You have always been our home" (Psalm 90:1, *Psalms for Modern Man*). In the midst of this present uncertainty, confusion and death we needed our God to be our home as He had never been before.

Our children would complete the year at Dalat School in two months so it seemed best to wait in Bangkok rather than go immediately to Canada. It soon became obvious that there was lots to do in the intervening time.

With the collapse of Cambodia hundreds of refugees were pouring into Thailand. The Canadian embassy opened an office to handle the resettlement of some in Canada. Norm's excellent command of the Cambodian language became a coveted skill and he spent many hours helping with formalities and filling out forms for those fortunate enough to qualify for immigration.

We also opened our home on Sunday afternoons to a small group of Cambodian Christians who wanted to worship the Lord. It was an informal time to both praise God and pour out our sorrows before Him.

One Sunday a young man dressed in the orange-colored robes of a Buddhist monk came through the door. We welcomed him warmly as he found a place in the circle of chairs. When prayer time was announced he bowed his shaven head with the others.

After most of the Christians had prayed and Norm was about to close the session the young man asked, "Can I pray, too?"

Hiding his surprise, Norm assured him that of course he could pray. Tears welled up in many eyes as we heard these words: "Oh God, in the past I thought I was a holy man but now I realize that I am a sinner and that it is only the blood of Jesus that can make me pure. Today I want to commit my life to Jesus. I will immediately remove these Buddhist robes and I will follow Him."

The room was electrified.

Norm discovered after the meeting that the man's name was Eang, a Cambodian presently living at a Buddhist temple in Bangkok. He had no clothes besides his robes, no possessions and no relatives in Thailand. He had permission to be in Thailand only because he was studying at the temple. Obviously he could no longer live there. His stock answer to any question about what he would do now was always the same, "That depends on the God who is the Lord."

Norm filled out forms asking to personally sponsor Eang to go to Canada and in June 1975 Eang arrive in Saskatoon, Saskatchewan, where he was lovingly welcomed by the Christians at Westgate Alliance Church.

In contrast to his clothes, bought at the Salvation Army Thrift Store, Eang always carried the biggest, most expensive Bible he could find. Every morning he rode his bicycle to the Kelsey Institute where he was enrolled in English classes.

One day as Eang tried to cross the road he was hit by a car. An ambulance took his broken body to the hospital but Eang never regained consciousness.

Norm was given the difficult task of conducting the funeral of this bright young man who seemed like a son to him. Though he had lived in Canada only four months, Eang had impacted many lives. Three hundred people filled the church for his funeral service.

At the close of the service, with tears brimming her eyes, his Catholic English teacher murmured, "he was a saint for heaven."

Eang was no doubt among the first to arrive in heaven as an indirect result of the devastation caused by Cambodia's fall to the communists. Who but our wonderful Lord could take a hor-

rendous, bitter circumstance and squeeze from
it sweet byproducts of everlasting delight?

# 19

## *Dararith and Chandara Come Home*

Darkness falls suddenly and early in Asia. As 6 o'clock approached on that rainy evening we were feeling very tired and very discouraged.

There was one more camp to visit but we questioned the wisdom of going there after dark, fearing the threat of communist sympathizers in the region. After some discussion, however, we decided that if we returned to Bangkok without checking out every possiblity we might later regret it.

Our mission on this trip was to pursue a request by Norm's sister and her husband in Canada to try to find two Cambodian orphan children they could adopt. So far on this day the answer was always the same, "There are no young children for adoption."

We arrived at the crude thatch reception office of the last camp well after darkness had fallen and trudged through the rain to meet the officials in their makeshift quarters. To our delight we also met the wife of Pastor Kong, a good friend from Cambodia, now being sheltered at the camp. We told her why we had come. Her response was immediate.

"Yes," she said, "we have a baby boy whose grandmother has decided to give him away. The baby's mother and grandmother are both here without their husbands. The grandmother has several little children of her own and does not think she can raise them all."

The officials refused to let us into the camp but agreed to allow us to meet the family there in the office. Soon a woman approached through the rain. A little bundle wrapped in a blanket was cradled in her arms. I took the child and peered into his tiny face. He was obviously underweight and had a cold. His mother, Bopha (not her real name), was not nursing him and, in the unsanitary conditions of the camp, bottle feeding might soon claim his life.

"Where is the mother?" I asked.

Someone ran to summon her and in a few minutes a pretty young woman appeared. Placing her baby in her arms we gently explained the reason for our visit.

"We definitely do not want to take your baby from you if you want to keep him," we said. "But if you have firmly decided to give him away we have a good home for him."

Bopha's hesitation was only momentary.

"Take him," she blurted, thrusting the bundle back into my arms. Evidently the baby was ours to keep.

We went on to explain that Norm's sister would prefer two children and asked if there were others. The mother pointed to a beautiful little four-year-old standing at her side.

"Would you take her, too?" she begged. "Then the two of them can stay together."

It was only later that we understood the full extent of the agony in that poor mother's heart. It was not lack of love that prompted her to part with her children. When the family had received the shattering news of the downfall of Phnom Penh, Bopha's husband, a police commissioner in a town near the border, had urged the family to flee into Thailand. He and his father would join them later that day after winding up a few business affairs. Sadly, the road was blockaded by the communists before they were able to leave. Neither was ever heard from again.

Bopha and her children, Chandara and Dararith, were totally dependent on the mother-in-law who saw them only as an unwelcome burden. She wanted Bopha to remarry so she would be rid of her. But remarriage for a woman with two dependents was a problem. Solution? Get rid of the children.

So the mother-in-law had made a decision. She would sell these beautiful children to a Thai. One shudders to think what might have happened to them, especially to that lovely little girl, if they had fallen into the wrong hands. Thailand's trade in prostitution is legendary.

Bopha had no recourse but to comply with her mother-in-law's wishes. When we arrived with our suggestion Bopha immediately recognized hope for her children's future. She would let them go to a good family in Canada.

"You will have a new family," Bopha explained to Chandara. "I want you to go to live with them. Don't think about me. Don't miss me."

We consulted with the camp officials about the next step.

"This camp is under the jurisdiction of the Thai governor of this province," we were told. "Before I can release the children to you, you will have to get a letter of permission from him. You will also need permission from the Ministry of Interior in order to take the children out of Thailand. I will give you a letter for the governor."

It was late Friday night. The governor would have long since finished his day's work and tomorrow his office would be closed. We were in a dilemma. We could hardly stay until Monday, but to go back to Bangkok and return the following week seemed equally difficult. With our problem still unsolved we committed the project to the Lord and sank into an exhausted sleep in our hotel room.

The next morning we sat down to eat breakfast in the hotel restaurant. Discovering that we were missionaries, the Christian hotel owner was extremely solicitous.

"Is there anything I can do for you?" he asked repeatedly.

Finally Norm replied, "Yes, there is. Can you tell me how to get in touch with the governor?"

"The governor?" he exclaimed, his eyes widening. "Why, he is sitting in the very next booth. He doesn't usually have breakfast here at the hotel but this morning he has a visitor from the Ministry of Interior. As soon as they have finished eating I will introduce you."

Norm and I looked at each other dumbfounded. The two men who could help us were right in the next booth!

After the usual polite greetings had been exchanged with the governor and his distinguished guest we presented our letter from the camp director. The governor read and pondered it for what seemed like hours.

Finally he said, "I am just trying to figure out how I can get a letter of permission typed up for you since my office is closed today.

"Waiter!" he snapped, "call my secretary at this number and tell him to hurry to my house. There is a letter that must be typed." Then, smiling at us, he invited us to follow him home. We sat down to chat with the governor's wife on the porch and within minutes the document was delivered into our hands. We thanked the governor profusely and left.

After a quick stop at the local market to purchase some vegetables for the refugees we drove
the short distance back to the camp. The director was most surprised to see us back so soon.

"I think we will have to meet with the governor," he commented hesitantly.

"Read the letter," we urged. "Doesn't it say
we can take the children?"

"Well, yes," the official agreed reluctantly.

And so the children were fetched and presented to us. Baby Dararith looked small and
pathetic, his little head half hidden by a woolen
cap. Chandara wore a little green sunsuit and
red boots. Her large dark eyes gazed at us
trustingly. We adored her from the start.

We suggested that the family need not send
along any extra clothes. We would get all that
was needed in the city. And so, with our good-
byes said, the four of us sped off for Bangkok
where we phoned Sophie and Jerry to tell them
the good news.

Then began endless legal proceedings. The
children needed permission to go to Canada,
permission that was not as easily obtained as we
had imagined. However, a friend at the
Canadian embassy worked with us to expedite
matters and when he was recalled to Canada he
continued to assist us in every way possible.

Sophie and Jerry already had an adopted
child so we reasoned that the long process of
home approval would have already been taken

care of. To our dismay we found out that all records are destroyed after 12 years. But once again, God intervened. Their documents had not been destroyed.

Chandara and Dararith filled our days in Bangkok with joyful activity. We bought only enough clothes to get them to Canada. I would often tell Chandara, "When you get to Canada your Mommy and Daddy will get that for you." She especially dreamed of having a doll like the ones she saw in the store windows and "pants with long legs."

As the day of our departure to Canada drew near we became increasingly apprehensive. Our own travel plans had been confirmed months before. We planned to take a tour of Israel and Europe with our children on the way home. But Chandara and Dararith were to go directly to Canada with Eang.

We prayed much for God's intervention and twice we made plans for their departure, only to send telegrams of cancellation because the visas had not arrived.

On the eve of our family's expected departure we read from our devotional book: "Now you can relax for I have done this mighty miracle for you."

*Was this really a promise from God for us?* we wondered. It seemed almost too direct, too good to be true.

The next morning our friend from the Canadian embassy called.

"The visas are here!" he announced joyfully.

In a flurry of activity the children were bundled off to the Thai embassy. Evening approached and with it closing time for the office. Miraculously the Thai officials consented to work overtime in order to get the paperwork ready, a unique occurrence in itself.

Within minutes of Norm's return from making the final preparations for Chandara and Dararith our own family climbed into the taxi that took us to the airport for our flight to Israel.

>⸺◆⸺◦⸺◆⸺<

Friends and family joined Sophie and Jerry as they excitedly awaited the arrival of the plane bringing their new children whose pictures they had carefully scrutinized. As the passengers deplaned Eang pointed to Jerry and whispered to Chandara, "That is your new daddy!"

Chandara dashed over to Jerry and threw her little arms around his neck. The little bundle that was Dararith was transferred to Sophie's welcoming arms.

Chandi and Darren were home.

# 20

# "I Give Them All to You"

It was a wonderful experience to arrive in Canada and be met by good friends who took us directly to a vacation cabin on the St. Lawrence River. We relaxed and soaked up the delicious fact that we were safely back in our own country.

Only a few months earlier I had prayed, my fingers poised on the typewriter, "Lord, I give all these things to You." Before me was a list of our family's possessions.

The list did not seem that long but it included all our household effects, all that had supported our lifestyle during the three-and-one-half years in Cambodia, all the things around which we had built precious memories. In two days we would be evacuated, leaving them all behind, for each person could carry only one small bag.

We were grateful to the Lord for His protection in those final days. We loved to recount how He had kept us safe and supplied our needs in a war-torn country. We had learned to trust Him. Still, we could not help but wonder about tomorrow. We had four children to provide for yet everything we owned would probably have fit in one small barrel. We had very little money and our future was uncertain.

"Honey," I said to Norm one day during our interlude in Thailand. "I can see people giving us some old furniture that they may have relegated to their basement family room, but who will give us the pretty things, like a beautiful lamp, for instance?"

There was only one answer—we would wait and see what the Lord had in store for us.

In the cabin next door to us on the St. Lawrence was a family from a nearby Alliance church. One afternoon the mother dropped by.

"Would you please watch my kids for a few minutes?" she asked. "I have to run an errand."

We agreed and it wasn't long until she returned with a big package.

"This is for you," she said, a smile creasing her face as she handed me the box.

Curiosity turned to delight as I gazed at the contents of the package. There in my hands was a beautiful lamp! We were not even home yet and already the Lord was beginning to shower us with His love gifts.

Someone else gave us money to buy dishes. Shelly and I were like two school girls as we bought a beautiful set with tiny flowers in her currently favorite color—pale purple. On our way out of the china department we passed the gorgeous imported bone china.

"Wouldn't it be nice, Shelly, if sometime we could have just a tea set in bone china?" It was not a request. It was not even a wish. It was just a comment.

We were sitting at the supper table one evening when some friends stopped by.

"We can't stay long," they said, "we just wanted to drop off this package."

Chris handed me a gift-wrapped box. With a little tug here and there the tissue soon fell away to reveal the translucent beauty of a bone china tea set—a teapot, cream and sugar, six cups and saucers and six little plates in the lovely American Beauty Rose pattern. Another gift from God's loving hand.

That summer we enjoyed every good thing He provided for us, but we realized that in stripping us of our possessions the Lord had accomplished something else—He had liberated us from the love of things that causes many to clutch their belongings tight-fistedly to themselves, anxious that they might one day lose them.

From that day we were free—free to enjoy the good things our loving Father provided, but remembering to hold them in an open hand.

# 21

## Capsized!

"**I** got one!" the excited cry resounded across the icy waters of Lake Delarond. There was no doubt about it. This fishing expedition was headed for success. Norm looked at his passengers, a happy smile lighting up his face.

Norm and the children—Rod, Doug, Shelly and David, ages 11 to 17—had dreamed about going fishing for many months. Happy memories of his own youth had prompted Norm to eagerly anticipate taking them far up into the Canadian wilderness where the beautiful clear lakes were ringed with pines and the isolation brought unequalled tranquility.

Finally the day came. Chattering excitedly the children piled into the car and headed for the lake. Behind them trailed the boat they had borrowed.

At the rustic fishing camp seasoned bewhiskered fishermen in plaid flannel shirts and blue jeans showed off their catches and joked about "the one that got away." Tomorrow *they* would be out on the lake and *they* would have something to talk about.

"If you really want the fish to bite you have to get up at the crack of dawn," counseled Norm out of his wealth of experience. However, the boat could not hold them all so it was decided that Shelly and Rod would sleep late while David and Doug accompanied their dad on the sunrise expedition.

When 4 a.m. approached Shelly and Rod burrowed deeper into the warm blankets as excited whispers emanated from the rousing fishermen. The door creaked shut and then in the distance the muffled roar of the motor could be heard.

Norm and the boys returned at 10 o'clock triumphantly showing off the magnificent fish they had caught. Shelly and Rod were more than eager to try their luck.

"Dave, how about taking Shelly and Rod out while Doug and I fillet the fish," Norm suggested. "Remember, we have to leave here at noon so be sure to be back by then."

Confidently David roared off with his passengers. The novelty of the event, the excitement of the catch, the vast expanse of solitude combined to create an unforgettable memory. Just how unforgettable they were about to discover.

Dave glanced at his watch.

"We'd better get back," he advised his younger siblings as he turned the boat and began to speed toward the shore. It was then they noticed that the once placid lake had suddenly filled with white caps.

Without warning, a huge wave abruptly capsized the boat tossing children, life-jackets, oars and gas tank into the cold gray water.

The children's hearts raced with terror as the icy waves washed over them. *In the event of an accident, stay with the boat.* They knew this was one of the fundamental rules for survival but this boat was not about to stay afloat. Slowly it sank from view.

Gathering their wits about them the children retrieved all that was left. David and Rod grabbed the lifejackets. Shelly draped herself over the bobbing gas tank. They overlapped the oars and all three clung to them so as not to get separated from each other.

Frantically they began swimming toward the shore but within minutes they realized they were making no progress for the wind was blowing away from the shore and they were being carried farther and farther out into the lake.

Above the noise of the wind and waves David shouted, "There's a cabin on the shore off to the right. Let's head for it." They all turned and paddled energetically in that direction.

David's feet were weighted down with heavy black army boots he had brought from Cambodia. But there was no way he was going to leave his priceless souvenirs at the bottom of Lake Delarond.

In an effort to keep their spirits up the children began to sing but the only songs that came to mind were songs about heaven. At one point Rod called to Shelly, "I think I just heard someone say, 'Well done.' "

On and on they swam toward a peninsula that jutted into the lake. Had they missed this finger of land they would have been swept out into another part of the lake in the rising storm.

After an hour of fighting the waves the children finally threw themselves on the shore. Though exhausted and freezing cold they decided to walk in the supposed direction of the cabin. They climbed up into the woods to be sheltered from the wind that now blew with a ferocity that seemed to have been held in check until that moment.

Back at camp Norm scanned the water. It was noon and there was no sight of the boat nor the children. As the wind continued to mount so did his concern. He hurried to the fishing camp office and asked an experienced boatman to scout the lake with him.

For an hour they circled the stormy waters. They saw nothing.

"We have to get back!" shouted the man. "This storm is getting dangerous." Choked with fear, Norm agreed. Just as they pulled up at the dock the wind tossed a boat onto the shore as if to mock them.

Norm and Doug looked at each other, apprehension filling their eyes.

"Let's pray, Doug," Norm suggested. It was

all they could do. They pled with God to keep the children safe. They tried to push down the stifling fear and replace it with trust but the sharp stabs continued to penetrate their thoughts.

Finally 12-year-old Doug spoke up.

"Dad, Jesus told me they would be all right." Was it just a childish hope or was it the voice of the Lord to a trusting heart? Time would tell.

An hour passed. The raging wind began to subside. The white caps settled. An old fisherman who regularly plied the waters catching fish for his mink ranch was seen venturing out. Norm called to him to swing around the lake to see if he could see the children.

Once again Norm and Doug waited and prayed, their eyes continually scanning the water. Suddenly they spotted the old fisherman's boat speeding toward them. As it neared the shore the man's hand shot up.

"I've got them!" he hollered.

*He's got them. What does that mean?* thought Norm, his heart in his throat. *Does he have the children or their bodies?*

Overwhelming, undescribable relief flooded over him as three tousled heads popped up and three grinning faces met his eyes. Tears mingled with lake spray as the children tumbled wearily out of the boat into the arms of their dad and brother.

Even today, I am convinced that our enemy, Satan, tried to take the lives of our children in that storm. But the Lord Jesus who was in charge of each one of them would not permit it.

After all, Jesus had said they would be all right!

## 22

# *Detour*

The collapse of Cambodia propelled us to another fork in our life's road. Our life's verse had promised that God would be our guide even unto death and we had always believed He had guided us to missionary service abroad. Now, after 15 years, were we to change direction? The thought was unsettling.

Norm and I spent much time in earnest prayer and serious reflection. On the one hand, were we not clearly called to be missionaries? That call had sustained us through many difficult days. Had it now terminated? Surely not! Staying home would be a cop-out, wouldn't it?

On the other hand, we had four teenaged children. Their lives had been bruised by the tumultuous events through which we had passed. They needed stability. David, now 18, struggled painfully as he sought to find a right relationship with others, with the Lord and with himself. Seeing his hurts, our hearts ached at the thought of leaving him in Canada to fend for himself. We felt it would be like throwing him to the wolves.

Norm and I did not habitually fast. However, the agony of our indecision and the needs of our children prompted us to spend one whole week fasting. It was absolutely imperative that we hear from the Lord.

First, God began to give us assurance concerning David. One morning while Norm was away on missionary tour and the children were all at school I again laid my burden at His feet. In conclusion I asked if He would send me a friend to come alongside to support me. I even dared to specifically ask that someone would phone and suggest we get together.

Anne Wahl heard the Lord's prompting in response to my prayer. A few hours later she called and asked if she could come over. In my heart I heard the whisper of the Holy Spirit assuring me that all my pleadings had been heard. *If the Lord would immediately answer the request for a friend to come visit,* I reasoned, *then the rest was sure to follow.*

Another day on my knees I again cried out to God for my firstborn. I reminded the Lord that He had created David in such a wonderful way. He had given him so many talents that were obvious to me.

Yet so much of what I knew to be there was hidden to the eyes of others as David jostled his way through bewildering adjustments. It seemed to me that this beautiful object of God's creation had somehow been dropped. Besmirched and sullied it lay in the mud. Those who passed

by glanced at it and, not recognizing its priceless value, gave it a kick and went on their
way.

Then the Lord gave me a mental picture of
what He planned to do. He showed me that He
would pick up this vessel He had made. He
would clean off all the mud and then He would
reshape it and engrave it with beauty. Vividly I
saw in my mind a beautiful golden goblet set on
a purple pillow. God's promises about restoring
Israel further encouraged my heart as I reasoned that what He did for Israel He could
also do for my son.

As our furlough drew to a close we were
being pressed to make a decision concerning
our immediate future. Just two months before
we would leave for the field, if that was to be
our decision, we were still vacillating.

On May 15 we kissed our children good-bye
and drove to the annual Council of The
Christian and Missionary Alliance. We shared
our confusion with close friends there and
inevitably received the same counsel: "Consider
the children's welfare."

On the last Sunday of Council we had a
meeting with Dr. Mark Lee, a well-known
speaker on the family. Before even hearing our
problem, he said, "Let me give you the priori-
ties: God comes first, your family second and
your work third. Now what is your question?"

"You have already answered it," exclaimed
Norm, his heart finally at rest.

As if to reaffirm the directions the Lord was giving, the district superintendent for our area asked to speak with us.

"I just received a telephone call from a group of people in Rosthern, a small town just north of Saskatoon," he said. "They want to join the Alliance and are asking for a pastor. Would you be willing to commit yourselves to serving them for a minimum of two years?"

A pioneer work in a predominantly Mennonite town was truly made to order for Norm, a missionary from a Mennonite background who had no recent experience in pastoral work. We returned from Council to go immediately to Rosthern.

The terrible events in Cambodia continued to grieve us deeply. Perhaps the burden would have been too heavy for us to carry. It seemed that God was withdrawing us for a time from Cambodian ministry and leading us to walk together through a pleasant valley of tranquility and healing.

Our hearts were quickly knit to the kind people in Rosthern. We were happy in the new house that our whole family had joined its efforts to create—picking the floor plan, hammering, painting, papering, laying carpet—and ultimately pronouncing our creation "very good"!

We were happy in the church among people who loved and appreciated us and responded joyfully to Norm's teaching and preaching. We watched in delight as they grew in the Lord.

We were also happily situated close to Norm's family. His mom and dad, sisters and their entire families often came to visit and enjoy oriental food. Cousins finally became acquainted.

David built himself a custom-made bedroom in the basement and found a job working for a member of the congregation.

For Doug and Rod, both junior highers, it was a big adjustment to be in a secular school after the hot-house atmosphere of a missionary boarding school. As young teenagers they were now obliged to confront intense pressure from their non-Christian peers. It was not easy to be known as "the kids whose dad is the new preacher in town."

Norm and I continued to scold, to love and to pray. It seemed to me that just at the time when our control over our children was beginning to slip away because they were growing up, the voice of the world was suddenly speaking too loudly and too persuasively.

As I talked the situation over with the Lord one day He once again brought comfort and assurance through His Word: "The one who is in you is greater than the one who is in the world" (1 John 4:4). I understood that since the Holy Spirit within Norm and me was greater, His voice speaking through us to our children would be more powerful and more persuasive than the voice of the devil coaxing them into the world. Since God was the greatest it would be He who would influence them for Himself, overcoming the weaker influence of the world.

The struggle between their Lord and the world was not always easy for our teenagers nor was their obedience to God always uncompromising, but their faith remained intact.

For the moment our path had turned away from missionary service, but this pleasant, flower-strewn path was but a brief detour before the next unpredictable chapter.

## 23

# *What an Exchange!*

In early spring of 1978 we received a letter from a former colleague in Cambodia. Jean-Jacques Piaget was now working with Cambodian refugees in France.

Because Cambodia was a former colony of France, refugees from that land had been given preferential treatment. Thousands had come to find shelter in the French reception centers. Among them were many Christians who had made a commitment to the Lord in the refugee camps in Thailand. Others not yet Christians were open to the gospel as never before.

"Would you consider coming to France for the month of May to tour the cities where there are Cambodians and to conduct a special retreat?" wrote Jean-Jacques. The idea intrigued us.

We were overjoyed when our church gladly gave their consent, considering that they were sending us on a missionary journey.

As we toured France we had the opportunity to pray with many refugees to receive the Lord Jesus as their Savior and little by little the emotional involvement with the Cambodian people that had been buried deep in our hearts began to resurface.

The heartbreaking stories that were poured into our ears again and again were met with a sympathetic response. We wanted so much to help ease the pain. There were so few Christian workers for Cambodians in France. The sole Cambodian pastor, Davy Ung, pled with us to come help him.

The climax of the trip came during the morning service of our last Sunday there. A young man from Lyon stood before those gathered for the retreat and confidently announced, "The Lord has promised that whatever we ask together in His Name He will do. We are now going to join together in prayer and ask that He send the Enses back to work with us in France!"

As Norm and I sat there surrounded by these earnest, loving petitions we were flooded with the intensity that always seems to accompany the certainty of God's will. After prayer we were invited to sing a duet. With tear-stained cheeks we faced those dear people who had suffered so much and now desired our help to show them how to begin a new life of meaning and purpose.

Trying to be at least somewhat objective we decided not to make a final decision about returning to France until we had gone back to Canada. But it seemed that both our family and our congregation knew that God's time for us in Rosthern had come to an end.

With a touch of sadness in his voice one of the elders confessed, "We knew when we let you go to France that you would not be staying with us."

Norm was compelled to immediately present his resignation but inwardly he wondered, *What's the rush?*

That question was answered on July 6 when we received a shocking call from our Mission office in New York. A car accident had just claimed the lives of the young pastor, Davy Ung, his wife and the daughter of one of the church elders.

Suddenly we understood why the Lord was rushing us to France. The Cambodian church was now in even more desperate need of spiritual guidance and comfort.

Leaving the warm comforts with which we were surrounded in Rosthern was not entirely without personal pain. Our family would be split up again—this time in three countries. We would be in France, David and Shelly would remain in Canada and Doug and Rod would attend the Black Forest Academy in Germany.

One Sunday in a service I bowed my head in prayerful submission. As all eyes around me were closed I raised my empty open hand to the Lord and said, "Lord Jesus, You can have it all. You can take from me whatever You desire. I give it all to You." Once again I knew in my heart that the pathway of obedience was the only way.

The next morning I busied myself with Monday morning chores, my mind flitting continually through the list of adjustments our family was facing. For some reason a certain chorus kept running through my head, "Abraham's blessings are mine. Abraham's blessings are mine. I am blessed going out and I'm blessed coming in, for Abraham's blessings are mine."

As I stuffed dirty laundry into the basement washing machine I wondered, *Why do I keep singing this song? What are these blessings I am singing about anyway?* I took a break and went searching for my Bible. Sitting down by the kitchen table I began to read from Deuteronomy 28: "If you will obey . . ." This phrase was followed by a wonderful litany of promises that would be the result of full obedience. I was especially drawn to the promise, "The fruit of your womb will be blessed."

Joyously and with a rush of excitement I bowed my head and said, "Oh yes, Lord! I do want all these blessings that You promise for obedience. I need not worry about my children if You will bless them."

My hand reached out as though to receive what He had promised to give. And then I realized that I was using the identical gesture I had used the previous day in church when I had surrendered all to Him.

*What an exchange!* I chuckled to myself and to the Lord. *His blessings for my obedience!*

# 24

# A House with a Yard

Another move! There were so many things to do to get ready. The house we had created with so much love had to be put up for sale. We had to pack up essentials and try to sell the rest. We had to say good-bye to dear friends who promised with tears to pray for us. We had to drive 1,200 miles to try to explain to my aged mother why we were going so far away from her. No doubt she sensed that we would not see each other again on this earth.

Less than a year later she was with the Lord but not before she had once again surrendered her rights to her children and grandchildren: "I gave you to the Lord before you were born and I'm not about to take you back now!" she affirmed repeatedly.

Finally, on the verge of departure we wrote a prayer letter to all our acquaintances. Prayer letters written at a time like that have a certain sameness about them. They plead for help with adjustments, with language and with housing. As I wrote, "Please pray that we might find a suitable apartment or house," the Lord seemed to ask, "Why do you pray for an apartment when you don't want an apartment?"

With a grin I energetically crossed out the word "apartment." What we really wanted was a house with a yard. We would trust the Lord for it.

In May during our one month tour in France we had stayed with Jean-Jacques and Maria Piaget in their charming old French house. It was surrounded by a small yard. Although suffering greatly from neglect it was evident that many years ago the garden had been lovingly laid out.

In one corner a huge weeping willow elegantly draped its graceful branches. Flower beds were outlined by beautiful rugged stones. Scattered throughout were roses and other flowers of many species.

The dining room windows could be swung open toward the garden and just in front of these windows was a trellis covered with bright scarlet roses and grapevines. Even then the pictures in my mind had revealed what a lovely home it could become for us.

The Piagets had vacated this house in June. It is unheard of for a dwelling of any size in the Paris area to remain vacant. Usually they are rerented within days. However, when we arrived in September we were overjoyed to discover that the Piaget's house was still available. The reason? It had too much furniture! Other potential renters apparently had plenty of furniture of their own. We had arrived with very little so access to the owner's furniture was an unexpected bonus.

For the first month after our arrival we busily feathered our nest in an intense need to re-establish a home. When it was all freshly papered and painted and a lovely color-coordinated rug covered the living room floor we invited the landlord to come.

With his delightful French accent he exclaimed, "I knew you would make it bee-oo-ti-fool bat I deed not theenk you would make it so-o-o-o bee-oo-ti-fool!"

Yes, it was a beautiful place, this home in Versailles. But its beauty was not in its physical structure but in its spiritual dimension. Throughout the 11 years we lived in that house God blessed many people.

The Lord has a wonderful promise for those who in order to serve Him leave loved ones behind and suffer the pain of loneliness. It is found in Mark 10:29-30: " 'I tell you the truth,' Jesus replied, 'no one who has left home or brothers or sisters or mother or father or children or fields for me and the gospel will fail to receive a hundred times as much in this present age (homes, brothers, sisters, mothers, children and fields . . . )' " God sent us hundreds of children, brothers, sisters, fathers and mothers to replace those we had left behind.

Cambodian brothers and sisters came. They came to enjoy the warmth of a home during those first months of difficult adjustment when their hearts were still raw and hurting.

They came to visit and to play. They came to pray and ask the Lord for direction. They came to study God's Word in their own language.

At Christmastime they crowded every corner of our living-dining room and spilled out into the hall and kitchen. A time of joyful singing, a feast of oriental food, a small gift exchange and games caused laughter that fairly shook the walls and created never-to-be-forgotten memories for both them and us.

One man expressed his thanks by saying, "This is the first time I have laughed since I experienced the terrible things that happened to me."

At a small group prayer meeting late one night a young man earnestly prayed for the salvation of his mother and father. Then, as the evening progressed, his real need surfaced. He finally confessed that legal documents with which he hoped to get to the United States to marry his sweetheart were filled with lies.

With God-given courage he was able to repent and make the necessary changes. He did not get to go to the United States nor marry that girl. But it was not long before his father and mother both became Christians.

For two years alternate weekends were devoted to a mini-Bible school. Potential church leaders from the Paris area joined students from the north of France. Norm and I took turns teaching them Bible, character development, church history and pastoral theology.

One vacation I stood at the dining room window and watched Doug and Rod hoisting huge rocks, working with their dad to construct an immense barbecue pit in one corner of the garden. It was large enough to hold 50 pieces of chicken at once. Our hearts danced with joy when on a warm summer evening every corner of the garden was filled with happy Cambodians enjoying spicy chicken, rice and salad topped off with great juicy slices of watermelon.

One day, many weeks earlier, as I had my personal devotions at a favorite spot in my beautiful garden, I had said to the Lord, "Lord, I want to give this garden to You but I don't know what the implications of that are." *How could He use a garden?* I wondered. As I surveyed that sea of happy faces some weeks later I suddenly knew.

>+◆+O+◆+<

In my kitchen is a huge bulletin board. Measuring 12 feet square it is crammed with prayer cards. Most of the faces that smile out at me are reminders of a happy encounter with people from all over the world that came to our Versailles home.

As each Christmas approached we would receive the inevitable letter. "I am in Europe this year. May I come for Christmas?" Every year the Lord sent us someone. We learned that it is far better to share our love with another lonely person than to pine for those who cannot be with us.

For the Christmas feast house guests were usually joined by local missionaries. It was no coincidence that I was the only missionary in Paris who had an oven big enough to hold a turkey roaster! Pictures taken year after year are all similar—a long table surrounded by faces brightened by candlelight and smiles.

The Lord had promised blessings in exchange for obedience. In the warm atmosphere of our Versailles "house with a yard" we enjoyed His blessings without number.

# 25

# *The Swellies*

Our roots had been yanked out of Canadian soil and replanted in Versailles, France, in great haste. Perhaps it was not surprising that we did not immediately flourish in our new environment.

We found ourselves pleading with the Lord for the blessings He had promised. We understood from His word to our hearts in Deuteronomy 28 that we would experience victory over our spiritual enemies, success in our work, His provision for all our needs and especially His blessing on our children.

We felt guilty for not being happier and for the turmoil that disrupted our hearts from one day to the next. Our guilt only increased when we compared our circumstances with those of our Cambodian friends. They had so little—we had so much, yet we were the ones who were miserable. The first winter in France was not a happy time in our lives.

By spring, however, after months of self-examination and struggling to find our place, we were finally beginning to feel at home in this new country and comfortable in the ministry

God had given us. It was not easy, particularly for me, but we decided to rejoice in the blessings we had already received and to trust God for the rest, confident He would keep His Word.

Mom and Dad Ens came for a visit and we proudly showed them around our part of the world. Soon David and Shelly also arrived and we all piled into the van for a relaxed and happy family tour of Europe.

It was then that I began getting what we jokingly called "the swellies." Hives—which are no joke—sprang out on various parts of my body and spread into enormous itchy red blotches only to fade and reappear elsewhere.

One night of the tour, at 3 a.m. in a charming little village hotel in Italy, I awoke with a choking sensation. My tongue had swollen to the size of a banana! I woke Norm. We prayed together but the swelling did not go down. I began to be concerned that my air supply might be cut off.

Quickly explaining to the children what had happened we hurried to the car. The deserted streets were lined with dark shuttered windows. Speeding toward the nearest city we were relieved to finally see signs pointing to a hospital. Of course, we knew no Italian but words were not necessary. I simply pointed to my huge tongue.

"Oh, *lingua*," said the orderly as if overgrown tongues were a common sight.

I was given a shot and then hooked up to

intravenous medication. It was not long until I felt the effects of the drug and the swelling subsided.

Back in Paris, not wanting to repeat the swellies adventure, I went through numerous allergy tests. All proved negative. The diagnosis, however, was not particularly comforting or entirely unexpected—my problem was the aftermath of a psychological crisis.

The doctor prescribed medication and as long as I faithfully took it I was fine. But as soon as I experimented taking myself off, the symptoms returned. What's more, I was frustrated and disappointed at our lack of ability to handle this situation through prayer.

The Alliance Women of our home district back in Canada happened to be sponsoring a unique project during that time. In order to become better acquainted with their missionaries they were asking various ones month by month to write an article on a given subject. My assignment was "Feelings." *How appropriate,* I thought to myself.

With all the honesty I could muster I shared the emotional upheaval I had experienced in adjusting to life and ministry in France and the unpleasant physical aftereffects it had triggered. There must have been strong, authoritative prayer warriors among those women for as they prayed I again attempted to go off the medication. This time the swellies did not return. Faithful prayer by others—not ourselves—

had pulled us through a difficult time.

Those women also began to pray for protection on the often windy, narrow and dangerous roads of Europe.

We loved to go to Switzerland. The majestic mountains seemed to draw our hearts close to their Creator and the sparkling snow evoked happy memories of our Canadian childhood. To make it all possible on a missionary budget, kind Christian people in a small Swiss mountain village offered apartments to missionaries free of charge.

Often when the two youngest boys were home on vacation from the Black Forest Academy we would take advantage of the wonderful skiing opportunities the Jura Mountains afforded. And after an exhilirating day on the slopes we would return wearily to our rustic apartment, enjoy a hearty supper, then spend an evening talking together, doing a puzzle or enjoying a starlit stroll—happy memories in the making.

So it was that we coaxed another missionary couple, Dr. Chuck and Becky Folkestad, and their family to join us for a post-Christmas break in our favorite vacation spot. Suitcase after suitcase, box after box was loaded into the van as we prepared for departure. Last of all the children filed into their places and we were finally ready to leave. As was our custom we bowed our heads in prayer and committed ourselves to our heavenly Father's protection.

I settled down into my seat in anticipation of the six-hour drive. We had just gone a few blocks when I suddenly thought to ask, "Honey, did you bring your ski jacket for me?"

"Why no," Norm responded, "I thought you would pack it."

Norm turned the van around and we headed home. I rushed into the house, picked up the jacket and within minutes was once again in my place and we were on our way.

It was a particularly foggy morning and visibility was poor as we swung onto the autoroute. We had not gone far when traffic came to a screeching halt. Ahead of us cars stretched for miles and soon several ambulances whined by.

For two hours we sat marooned wondering just what terrible tragedy could cause such a long delay. The television news that evening explained it all. Two cars had collided in the fog and an additional 16 vehicles had piled into them forming a horrendous fiery heap of metal.

When the debris was finally cleared from the road, traffic was again allowed to proceed. We glanced at our watches. As we came upon the evidence of the accident we looked at each other in amazement—we had driven 10 minutes—just about the amount of time our little detour for the jacket had taken!

We were convinced that God had used a forgotten jacket and the prayers of faithful people to protect two missionary families that wintry day.

There never seemed to be enough hours in a day. I often rushed from one thing to another often feeling I should be accomplishing more. Rod saw my anxious bustling about one day and gently reprimanded me, "Slow down, Mom!" Time and again his admonition echoed in my mind. Still I continued to drive myself thinking the Lord would surely be more pleased with me if I did more for Him.

Then one day He showed me in a most poignant way that our relationship was based on far more than my trying to work for Him.

We had been invited to a Cambodian engagement ceremony. An atmosphere of quiet joy pervaded the room as the guests and the future bridegroom sat on mats on the floor listening to the customary speeches.

Then the moment came for the bride to be brought into the room and presented to her fiance. She was a stunningly beautiful young woman. Her hair was arranged in lovely curls and her face had a glow that came from more than the make-up that her friends had so painstakingly applied. Her dress was dark green silk; its long skirt carefully pleated.

As she entered the room I leaned over to Norm.

"You know," I said, "we should look lovely like that for Jesus. As part of the Church we are engaged to Him."

The next day, Sunday, we attended a French worship service. I could hardly believe my ears as the pastor announced the subject of his message: "We are engaged to Jesus!"

The message was tailor-made to my need as tenderly the Lord Jesus showed me that He was not an exigent taskmaster always demanding a bit more of me than I could effectively produce. Rather, He was the One who loved me with utmost compassion and delighted to care for me even as a young man cares for his sweetheart.

At the end of the service we sang a chorus over and over again—"Jesus, mon Bien-Aimé"—"Jesus, My Beloved." I realized that what God wanted was not busy bustling but the love of an undivided heart.

I was at peace.

## 26

# God Keeps
# His Promise

"She makes me happy all the time." We could not argue with that statement as we shared Rod's joy over the special friend he had found. Having met her we agreed that Cindy was a lovely young woman. But there was one problem—Rod and Cindy were in 10th grade!

The authorities at the Black Forest Academy understandably frowned on serious relationships between students so young. But time proved that Cindy was indeed a special blessing from the Lord for Rod. Their high school romance bore the test of time and separation as Cindy headed to the States and Rod to Canada after graduation. It also bore the test of obedience as both sets of parents suggested they wait an extra year before getting married.

One evening out of the blue Norm asked, "Why is it we are insisting those kids wait a year to be married?"

Neither of us knew the answer to that question except that they would be a year older. In the meantime they would be sad and lonely, separated from each other and from their missionary parents in France and Spain.

The next morning Norm called Rod over to him.

"Rod, if Cindy's parents will give their consent for you two to marry this year, so will we."

With a great deal of trepidation Rod prepared himself for the phone call to Cindy's father. Every question his future father-in-law could possibly ask was carefully thought through and written down with an appropriate answer. And sure enough—he was to need all those answers.

Apparently the answers were the right ones, for consent was given for Rod and Cindy to marry.

"If you obey, the fruit of your womb will be blessed," the Lord had promised me that day in Rosthern. God had indeed blessed Rod through bringing us to Europe. He was keeping His promise.

>─┼◆─O─◆┼─<

"Where do you come from?" someone asked Doug, our youngest. "Well, um, I was born in Cambodia, lived in Thailand, went to school in Malaysia, my parents are Canadian, but now they live in France and I go to school in Germany."

It was soon time for Doug to graduate from the Black Forest Academy and return to

Canada. At the airport we checked his baggage then found a place to sit and wait for the plane that would carry our son away.

"Well, Doug," commented his dad breaking an awkward silence, "you have gotten on and off planes many, many times in your life, haven't you?"

We began to count the times Doug had crossed a border from one country to another beginning with his first flight from Cambodia to Thailand when he was 20 months old. He was now 17 years old. The startling total was 60 border crossings.

If we had been able to look into Doug's future at that moment we could have added his stint in the Philippines and Hong Kong working with refugees, his year of study at Bodenseehoff, Germany, where he met his wife Jane; their making a home in California near the Mexican border, their studies in New York, California and North Carolina which produced a doctorate in psychology for Jane and a doctorate in English for Doug.

"I will bless your children," God had promised. He was in the process of keeping His word.

>─╍◆╍─O─╍◆╍─<

Does a child ever get so old that his or her parents are no longer concerned? Probably not!

After all our children were grown and scattered around the world we continued to pray and sometimes to worry. The Lord used an unusual incident to convince me that I did not have to worry, but only to trust Him, for had not we entrusted our children to Him?

Norm's parents had given me a beautiful gold and black pen. One particular day I spent much of the afternoon at the kitchen table answering a stack of letters. As supper time approached I quickly gathered up the papers and old envelopes that lay scattered over the table and stuffed them in a garbage bag.

Later that evening Norm took the bag to the street for pick-up. On an impulse he tossed it across the road to where the neighbors had piled their bags. He missed the pile and the bag hit the curb. As he went to pick it up he spied something sharp poking through the bag. Curious, he bent down to investigate. Sure enough—it was my favorite pen.

When Norm came back to the house he just smiled and handed me the pen. But at that moment the Holy Spirit spoke to me: *If God cares so much about something as insignificant as a pen, will He not also care for your most precious possessions, your children?* With hundreds of miles separating us we as parents obviously did not know their needs, their situations, their problems even as I had not known about the pen. But God knew. And yes, we could trust Him to take care of our children.

I was learning that He was a God who kept His promises.

## 27

# Camp of Death . . . and Life

Into the terrible darkness of the cruel rule of the notorious Pol Pot burst a ray of light and hope in January, 1979—Cambodia was invaded by Vietnam.

In the ensuing disruption tens of thousands of Cambodians took the opportunity to flee their communist slave masters. Emerging from the forest bordering Thailand they arrived in droves, emaciated, terrified, heartbroken, each with his or her own personal horror story.

Refugee camps were quickly erected and aid from the entire world poured in to save these lives who had become the most pitiful and pitiable people on earth.

The Christian and Missionary Alliance, through its relief arm—CAMA Services—immediately sent a medical team to Sakeo Camp up on the Thai/Cambodian border. We were called to join them as chaplain and interpreters. With our minds still in a whirl we found ourselves leaving Paris and winging our way to Bangkok. Accompanying us was a young Cambodian

woman from New Zealand named Thavy
Ngeth.

Arriving at the Alliance guest home in
Bangkok we met the Dutch medical team, a
capable collection of nurses and support staff
headed by a Salvation Army captain. She curt-
ly informed us that Sakeo was a Khmer Rouge
(communist) camp and that we would not be
permitted to do any evangelizing. But even
before we saw them we knew that these bro-
kenhearted people had needs that no amount of
medical assistance could meet.

We were up early the next morning eager to
be on the road to the border but it was late
afternoon before we finally reached Sakeo
Camp.

Emotions of all kinds flooded our hearts and
minds as we drove past barbed-wire fences and
through a checkpoint manned by armed Thai
soldiers. Before us stretched a sea of small blue
plastic tents each supported by a single stick. A
long trench sprinkled with lime provided the
only sanitation facilities.

The food distribution tent was empty but
tomorrow a long line would form as everyone
waited patiently for the day's supply of rice
and vegetables and meat. The shame of being
reduced to beggars was overcome by gratitude
at having their interminable hunger at long
last assuaged.

We gazed longingly at these Cambodians
whom we loved. What a contrast to the beau-

tiful people we had left in that delicate land in
1975. All about us were grim, unsmiling faces.
The black cotton clothes required by Pol Pot still
draped the tired and emaciated bodies of both
men and women. All the young girls had their
beautiful black hair cropped short. Everywhere
we heard the hack of terrible coughing.

"Come to the hospital," someone urged us.
Six huge canvas tents had been hastily erected
to accommodate the thousands of sick people.
In fact, nearly everyone at Sakeo Camp was
ill. The hospital cared for only the most desperately ill. Straw mats, laying on the rain-
soaked ground, were the only beds.

Darkness was falling and after a brief tour we
were told to leave quickly and get ourselves
settled in the Alliance house just outside the
camp. Tomorrow would be time enough to get
involved, they said. It was hard to leave—right
now we wanted to do something, anything, to
ease the awful suffering that engulfed us.

We were warmly welcomed to the rented
quarters by Aree, a former cook from the guest
home in Bangkok and taken to the dining room
were she had prepared a delicious meal. The
house was built on pillars creating a pleasant,
breezy cement-floored dining room under the
sleeping area. Meals were served to the accompaniment of nature's music: birds, crickets,
barking dogs, crying babies. Little lizards and
an occasional toad also graced us with their
presence.

Physically and mentally exhausted by the trip and the sights of Sakeo Camp we were relieved to be directed upstairs and given plastic air mattresses. Another couple who had abandoned their medical practice in Sao Paulo, Brazil in exchange for six weeks of ministry here also joined us.

We blew up the brightly colored mattresses and joked about the order in which we should place them in the allotted space, finally settling on having the women sleep in the middle, with the men on each side. On the floor beside us we arranged the contents of our suitcases.

Thavy, the New Zealander, was given her mattress and directed to sleep beside the screen door that was all that protected us from real or imagined terrors of the night.

In the middle of the night, Thavy, herself a refugee from similar terrors to which she was now being reintroduced, awoke in great alarm convinced that the late night roar of motorcycles on the road was the sound of approaching Khmer soldiers.

Morning brought a measure of peace and Thavy showed great courage and love for her people by remaining with the team. Long after the rest of us were gone she continued to minister victoriously in the camps.

We climbed into the back of the Toyota van and headed back to Sakeo Camp. Pausing for a moment in the little cubicle near the entrance flap we united our hearts in an earnest plea for

God to work through us, to give the strength of spirit and body that we so desperately needed, to bless the medical staff with wisdom and to bring these sad, suffering people physical and spiritual health. Then we went out to face the most appalling scenes we had ever witnessed.

Doctors, accompanied by nurses and an interpreter, crawled slowly along the rows of mats, asking questions and administering drugs that had been abundantly supplied by sympathetic people around the world. Yet in spite of the help many of the patients were just too weak to benefit. The dead were simply rolled unceremoniously in their mats and taken to another tent where the floor space was filled with the grisly reminders of the realities of war.

There was no time for a decent burial and even if there had been time, many of the dying had no relatives with them. They slipped from their weary lives leaving only a commonly held first name—Sok or Peng or Ung—to identify them. Periodically a truck came and cleared the tent, taking the bodies to a common grave somewhere in a remote field.

>—+—◦—+—◦—+—<

A motherless 12-year-old sat with his critically ill father in the hospital tent where Norm worked. Day after day he sought to help the nurses care for his only remaining parent. But sadly one day the father could no longer fight for his life.

"Marie," a nurse called, "come see if there is

something you can do to help this child."

I was met by a youngster with the impassive face of one who has known more suffering than any little boy should be called upon to experience. Dry-eyed he led me to his little plastic tent home. I put my arm around his thin shoulders as I walked beside him, at a loss for words.

"Dad died," he muttered to his little brother squatted in the stifling heat of the tiny tent. What was there to say? What was there to do but pray? Gathering my wits, I poured out our sorrow to the Lord Jesus, begging Him to take care of these orphans.

When I finished a small tear was finally making its way down the brown cheek of the brave little boy.

><+>+O+<+>+<

"We can't find my husband," cried the woman from her mat, anxiety clouding her eyes. She herself was sick and unable to search for her husband but her grown children had been making the rounds from one hospital tent to another. Their search to this point had been futile.

"Give me his name," I suggested, "and we will look for him together."

At the admissions tent I asked, "Did you admit a man on November 14 by the name of Sok?"

The thumbworn notebook was taken from its dusty shelf and the orderly ran his finger down the list of names under November 14.

"Yes," he exclaimed. "Here it is. Oh, I'm sorry—that man died here in the admissions tent before he could be treated."

The family and I wandered wearily back to where the mother lay. How we would have loved to cheer her with happy news instead of having to tell her she would not see her husband again.

Bravely they thanked me for my help. "At least we know for sure what happened to him and that eases our minds," they commented with heartbreaking resignation.

⊱┈❖┈◦┈❖┈⊰

A young woman lay dying on her thin mat. Her gaunt face gave evidence of the sickness and starvation she had endured. Troubled eyes searched mine as I knelt to talk to her. She was unable to respond, too ill to voice what was in her mind and heart.

With utmost simplicity I shared with her the love of the Lord Jesus Who would take away her sins if she would just ask Him and would welcome her to the heaven He had prepared.

"I will pray to Him now," I told her. "If you agree with me, you pray, too, in your heart."

Quietly she listened as I expressed a desire for forgiveness and acceptance by the God of heaven. I smiled once more into her eyes and left to help others.

When I returned a little later she weakly raised her hands in the traditional Cambodian greeting. Words were not necessary as her eyes revealed the peace she had found. Later that day I paused before an empty space where her mat had lain. I had shared Christ with her just in time.

>—·—‹›—·—○—·—‹›—·—‹

Our emotions were like a yo-yo as we sometimes shared heartbreak, at other times overwhelming joy.

"See if you can help this mother find her baby," came the request one day.

Reaching gently toward the woman I invited her to come with me. "We'll check at the intensive feeding unit first," I said.

As we walked toward the tent I asked numerous questions, my heart sinking deeper and deeper with each answer.

"She was three years old, my baby.

"She was very sick so they took her away from me when they put me on the bus coming here.

"She couldn't walk yet. She was too weak.

"I was still nursing her."

*What hope was there,* I wondered, *of finding such a child alive?*

Hope faded further as we found no trace of the little one at the feeding unit. Raising a cloud of red dust we shuffled past other tents of the pediatric unit staffed by doctors and nurses from France. I explained our plight but no one had seen a child that matched the description.

"Go ahead and walk through the ward," suggested a nurse. "Maybe you will see the baby you are looking for."

Slowly we wandered from bed to bed, looking, looking, looking. In the midst of our despair an excited voice called out, "Auntie, your baby is here!" We ran toward the voice and my eyes brimmed with tears as mother and child reached eagerly for each other.

>–+–‹›–0–‹›–+–‹

One morning I was asked to interpret at the outpatient clinic where gravely ill patients were given an admission slip to the hospital and all others were handed medicine and sent back to their tents. It seemed to me that morning that nearly everyone qualified for hospital care so I quickly wrote out one admission slip after another.

Suddenly a nurse from the admissions tent came rushing over.

"Stop! Stop!" she cried. "We can't keep up. You are sending us far too many people. You will have to come and tell some of them to go back home."

My heart was heavy as I surveyed the crowd of people I had just sent over there. Sick as they were they had spent three hours squatting patiently in the hot sun waiting for help. Now I would have to tell them they could not have it because they were not sick enough.

Thankfully an Israeli doctor arrived and touching each patient announced, "This one is sick; this one can go home. This one is sick; this one can go home."

Coming to one woman, he said, "She can go home." I whispered the distressing news to her in Cambodian.

The woman looked up at me with pleading eyes.

"Someone will have to help me," she said quietly. "I can't walk."

It was more than I could take. At that moment all the pent-up sorrow and sympathy accummulated over days of witnessing this human tragedy suddenly broke from my heart.

"I can't do this," I blurted, the tears pouring in torrents down my cheeks. Hastily I excused myself and made my way to the nurses station. I lingered there until my soul had been emptied, till no more tears would fall.

><+•·O·•+><

Lang, a thin weary woman, worked in the hospital tent where Norm was interpreting. She came to him one day in intense distress.

"Pastor, you must get me out of this camp!" she cried. "Last night I saw the murderers of my children right here!"

When the Khmer Rouge had marched into Phnom Pehn that long ago day in 1975, Lang's husband had been a capable doctor, her sons promising teenagers and her daughter an adorable little child. Her husband had been summarily executed as were all educated people. Then, with her children, Lang was taken to a commune where her agony was only compounded. Her sons were taken out and killed, probably by a blow from a bamboo stick to the back of the neck.

Lang knew she was being watched. She knew that if she showed grief she would be judged as sympathizing with the opposition and executed as well. Thinking of her little daughter who still needed her she hid the anguish of her heart and continued on with life as if nothing had happened.

Lang had felt safe in Sakeo Camp. But the real truth was that although she had escaped Cambodia she had not yet escaped the presence of her enemies. In response to her plea Norm promised to do his best to get her to Canada. But before those negotiations were completed we heard the happy news that Lang was safely in New Zealand.

⊳—⊢⟨⟩—O—⟨⟩⊣—⊲

Cautiously, aware of the admonition against evangelizing, Norm offered a group of men a gospel tract. "God" the title boldly proclaimed in Cambodian. Equally cautious hands reached for the inviting little piece of paper but soon people were swarming around Norm grasping eagerly for reading material so long denied them.

To our delight we realized that the only reading materials in the camp were the hundreds of tracts and Gospels of John which we now imported into the camp each day. The administrators of Sakeo Camp might well be Khmer

Rouge, we finally decided, but the people were simply Cambodians with hearts starved for a spiritual dimension in their lives. It was not long until Norm had his first camp convert.

Our six weeks came to a close and our hearts were torn as we returned to Paris. It seemed that the needs of these camps were of far greater importance than those of the people of Paris. Yet we knew that the newly arrived refugees in France needed shepherding, too.

Six months later the call came once again for another six-week stint in the camp. We accepted with eager anticipation.

What changes greeted us! In those six months school buildings had been built and children were happily learning their Cambodian characters. We were touched to witness a return to traditional culture, to colorful clothing, to joy and playfulness. The hospital was still there but the number of sick people was already greatly reduced.

The fledgling church we had left in the camp was now strong and growing and more were being added daily to the number who called themselves Christians. Hospital tents had been replaced with more permanent thatch buildings. Several of these now stood vacant and after much persuasion we were allowed to use one as a church.

Every day Norm would teach the "old" Christians—those who had accepted Christ more than a week ago—and I would teach the new believers. We had only one building, so Norm and I would stand back to back with our students in front of us. The floor was made of crushed rock, so to add to their comfort the people would take off their rubber thongs and sit on them sometimes for hours at a time.

Periodically Norm officiated at a Christian wedding. A space was cleared between the rows of blue plastic tents and two battered chairs placed there for the bride and groom. First the bridegroom arrived looking solemn but perspiring profusely in his dark suit, white shirt and tie he had borrowed for the occasion.

Then his shy, unsmiling bride, decked out in traditional country Cambodian wedding garb— a bright red dress ornately decorated, a garland of shiny gold ornaments in her beautifully arranged hair, her face unfamiliar with its uncustomary layer of make-up—would join him.

A little table in front of them was adorned with a vase of plastic flowers carefully saved from previous ceremonies. Beside it was a Bible and three candles. Also prominently displayed were big bottles of Coke and orange sodas, an indication of just how special this event was.

A music group from the church crowded behind the bride and groom and I suspected that the Lord smiled at their unique praises. We certainly did.

The short ceremony was followed by a meager wedding feast made from food distributed in the camp or bought with a carefully hoarded

bit of money. Even if a honeymoon had been a
part of their culture there was no way to get
past the barbed-wire perimeter of the camp.
The couple's honeymoon suite was a tiny blue
plastic tent in a long row among hundreds of
others.

So life went on. Babies were born, some of
whom were destined to spend the next 12 years
of their lives behind those same barbed-wire
fences. Others welcomed the day when they
boarded a plane for France, the United States,
Canada, New Zealand and other faraway
places.

Families were split up never again to be
reunited. Their one desire was to find shelter
somewhere in a country where they could live
their lives in peace and freedom.

In the hollow of His hand.

Norman and Marie, Wedding, 1956.

Leaving for boarding school; Shelly with Baby Secret.

Rod (middle of picture) stands where the rocket fell; Marie and the other children gaze from the front gate.

Tom and Sandi Wisley with the Enses at Buriram.

A spirit house in Thailand.

Church meeting under a Cambodian house.

Noah's Ark Church, 1974

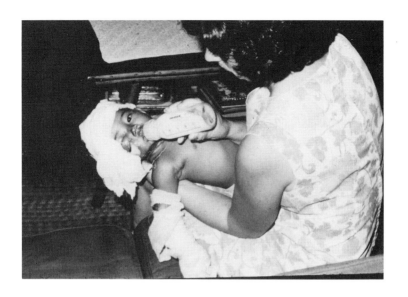

Marie with the daughter of "the survivor"who was severely burned.

"The survivor" with her husband and daughter. Her daughter died
during the Pol Pot regine.

The crazy lady.

Ens kids leaving Phnom Penh for Dalat School in Penang, Malaysia.

Baboo and daughter of "the survivor."

Baboo

Candi and Darren in their new home.

The house in Versailles.

Sakeo Camp—35,000 people sheltered under blue plastic tents.

Church at Sakeo Camp.

Wedding at Sakeo Camp.

David and Yeang at city hall for the civil ceremony required in France for all weddings.

Norm leads singing with his guitar.

Sopheap who was healed and is now pastoring one of the Cambodian churches in Paris.

Marie and her family at a reunion, summer 1993.

## 28

# The Sickness of Sopheap

Sopheap clutched his stomach and groaned. The pain he had experienced so frequently in the past had returned. Slowly he made his way to the Buddhist temple and explained his symptoms to the old priest who sat placidly, clad in his faded yellow robes.

The priest rose and shuffled to another room to get the paraphenalia he needed to perform the ceremony that would bring a cure for Sopheap. He returned with a bowl of water and a branch of leaves.

Sopheap bowed his head and closed his eyes. He felt the cool droplets of water as they were sprinkled on his fevered brow. He listened absentmindedly to the chant intoned in words he did not understand.

"Go home now and rest," instructed the priest. "You will be well."

Sopheap found his way home and lay down on the mat which covered his hard wooden bed. Soon he was sleeping peacefully. When he awoke the pain and fever were gone. He felt well and strong.

This procedure was repeated over and over and always the water-sprinkling ceremony and the incantations of the Buddhist priest brought welcome relief.

On one of these visits a priest confidently announced, "I know why you continually get sick. It is because someone has put a spell on you and I know who it is because I dreamed about her last night."

The priest commenced to describe a young woman whom Sopheap immediately recognized.

"I can relieve you of your problem permanently," the priest assured him. But once again the priest's ministrations brought only temporary relief.

The day came when Sopheap's village was taken over by the dreaded Pol Pot regime. One night Sopheap decided the time had come for his escape. Taking with him the images of the gods he trusted he snuck quietly out of the village. It was not long before he was in the dark forest that lay between him and the Thai border. He wandered there for several days, his strength slipping away with each plodding step.

Soon Sopheap realized that he was hopelessly lost. Desperately he prayed to the gods he carried with him, but as the day wore on he realized that these gods either could not or would not help him. Disgusted, he left them in the hollow of a tree and continued on his way.

Then he remembered a conversation he had had with a Buddhist friend some years earlier. The friend had told Sopheap, "When the Christians pray they say, 'Our Father in heaven.'" Now, lost, hungry and afraid, Sopheap cried out, "Oh, Father in heaven, please help me find my way out of this forest!" It was not long until he discovered the path that led to the border.

Arriving there he found himself at a Thai army camp.

One day, a scrap of paper on the ground caught his eye and he picked it up.

"Oh," he exclaimed, "this is a page from the Christian Bible!" Carefully he smoothed out the wrinkles, gently folded the paper and placed it in his pocket.

Nearby was Khao I Dang refugee camp, ringed with barbed wire and guarded by armed Thai soldiers. No one was allowed in or out. Yet in spite of restrictions messages had a way of reaching their intended receivers.

The news was whispered to Sopheap one day that a man had died in the camp. His friends would neglect to report the death to the authorities, Sopheap was told, and he could take the man's place.

Under the inky cover of night Sopheap slipped into the camp and he was given the man's identity papers along with a new name and age.

In that camp those who had the right to call God "Father" were enthusiastic about their faith. Soon they contacted Sopheap and invited him to listen to the gospel in the thatch church building in the center of the camp. Sopheap accepted their invitation and joined the group on the rough-hewn benches in the dirt-floor structure.

The singing was awesome, the tunes often familiar Cambodian folk songs, but the words filled with the joy of knowing the Father in heaven. Sopheap immediately responded to the invitation to accept Jesus as His Savior and Lord.

It was not long before Sopheap's old sickness was back.

*Oh, no,* he thought, *What will I do now? Since I am a Christian I can't go to the Buddhist priest and be sprinkled.* Then, realizing his privileges as a child of God, he said to himself, *I know what I will do—I will pray and ask the Lord to heal me.*

In simple, childlike trust Sopheap committed his sickness to his heavenly Father in Jesus' name. The sickness left as it always had before. But this time there was one important difference: it never again returned.

# 29

# *Kill the Fatted Fish*

On our visit to Thailand we received news that developed into a wonderful answer to prayer. David, our oldest, was being offered an opportunity to work with CAMA Services in Sakeo Camp. Norm and I were, of course, hoping for his quick arrival so that we could spend as much time with him as possible. But it seemed that God had something more important on His agenda, for spiritually David was not yet ready for ministry.

One evening in Saskatoon David attended a service where the speaker was Ravi Zacharias whom he had met before at Dalat School. That night David heard the well-known story of Jonah and how God had spoken to him but he had disobeyed. David thought of his own life and of his own disobedience to God. At the invitation he made his way to the altar.

"Hello, David!" said Ravi while a far greater Voice echoed the words, "Hello, David!" and the angels in heaven rejoiced as David surrendered his life anew to Christ.

Our time in Thailand overlapped with David's arrival by only a few days. What a reunion it was—God was keeping His promise to bless our children. How grateful we were!

We managed to find time to enjoy a "prodigal-son-come-home" meal together at a restaurant in Bangkok. As we savored the delicious seafood we laughed and joked about having killed not the fatted calf but the fatted fish.

Two very happy parents returned to their room at the guest house that night. Before going to sleep we knelt by the bed and praised the Lord together. Many years earlier God had made us a promise, a promise of restoration for David. Now that promise had been fulfilled. God had indeed picked up our son and cleaned him up and was in the process of shaping him to be a vessel He would delight in.

David had always had a special love for the Cambodian people. At the impressionable age of three he had first come to live in their beautiful country. When he left for school in Malaysia he filled his lonely intervals dreaming of how wonderful it would be to return to Cambodia. Home, Mom, Dad and Cambodia were all synonymous in David's heart and mind.

When David completed his service in the camps he returned to Canada where he was encouraged to complete his Bible school training to prepare him for ministry to Cambodians. Spurred on by such a hope David re-enrolled at Canadian Bible College.

His summers were spent with us in France.

One memorable week David discovered that God can overcome even distance and cultural barriers in the accomplishment of His will.

The Cambodian family camp was meeting. From all over France they had come to spend a week together in fellowship and study of God's Word. Among them were two teenaged sisters, No and Yeang Pak, who had just recently arrived from Khao I Dang camp where they had learned about the Lord. Now they eagerly responded to the opportunity to be with fellow Christians again.

In the relaxed family atmosphere of the camp David and Yeang quickly became acquainted. On the drive home the car was filled with laughter as No and Yeang taught David the Cambodian version of "Old McDonald Had a Farm"—"My Grandfather Has a House in the Country"—accompanied by strange and hilarious animal sounds.

When David returned to Canada after the summer with us he realized he had left his heart in France. The sweet face of Yeang Pak filled his waking thoughts. The next time he came to France, he decided, a visit to the little town of Epinal would be first on his list!

The following year David returned to France and true to his word he headed for Epinal. The visit was eminently successful and the whole Pak family was charmed by this handsome young Canadian who amused them with funny stories told in fluent Cambodian. Then all too quickly it was time for David to return to Canada and letters began to criss-cross the ocean that now separated Yeang and David.

"Let's go for a walk," I suggested to Yeang one day on a visit to Epinal. Strolling along together I cautiously quizzed her about her relationship with David.

"Are you just writing letters to each other for fun?" I asked rather pointedly.

"Oh, no," she responded. "We love each other and want to be married."

David expressed the same sentiments—we would have a Cambodian daughter-in-law! *Just imagine, I thought, one day I will hold in my arms a little Cambodian and it will be my own grandchild!*

Seeking to proceed with utmost propriety Norm and I drove to Epinal to arrange for the marriage. Yeang's older brothers and sister all gathered for the momentous occasion. Sitting in a circle in their home the two families mutually decided that it was a good match. Yeang was there quietly listening but not participating in the conversation. It was decided that when David came to France the following summer we would have an engagement ceremony.

What a cultural event that was! Some of the Christians from our church helped us purchase the customary gifts of fruit and sweets. These were meticulously arranged in pairs on round metal trays then wrapped in red cellophane. Traditional gifts for a Cambodian bride-to-be were replaced by the traditional gift of David's culture—an engagement ring.

Memories of long-ago engagement ceremonies in a more primitive Cambodia called for a joyous procession of merrymakers making their way down a dusty road bearing the groom's gifts to the bride who sat secluded in her thatch or wooden house.

Uncharacteristically we parked our cars beside the highrise apartment where Yeang lived with her mother. The women had donned their most beautiful Cambodian skirts and lace blouses, the men their suits and ties. We lined up in procession and the colorful trays were distributed. To the accompaniment of much camera snapping we slowly made our way to the apartment elevator.

The bride's family and friends welcomed us with huge smiles and the traditional Cambodian greeting of upraised clasped hands. We were ushered into the living room which had been cleared of all furniture and were invited to sit on mats on the floor. Our tray gifts were arranged in the center of the mats.

Friends and family of the groom were seated on one side of the room. Facing them on the other side were the bride's family and friends. The spokesman for our family was an elder from the Cambodian church in Boulogne. He pointed out that we had brought gifts and hoped they were acceptable.

Finally Yeang was ushered in from the bedroom where she had been sequestered. She looked truly gorgeous. Her long maroon-colored silk dress was woven with silver threads. Her hair was beautifully set and her face made up with utmost care and attention.

Shyly she took her place on the mat beside David. He placed his ring on her finger and she responded by presenting him also with a gold ring. A feast was enjoyed by all.

The following summer David returned to Paris to marry Yeang and to take her back to Canada with him.

Then in 1990 David and his family joined the missionary staff in France. Our joy was boundless. David had come to be the business agent, a misnomer which really means "servant of all."

One day sitting in bed propped up by pillows and with my early morning cup of coffee in my hand and my Bible open before me, I read these words: "The greatest among you will be your servant." I smiled as my thoughts flew back to the mental picture the Lord had given me years earlier. That vision of a beautiful vessel on a purple pillow—David—was being fulfilled before our very eyes.

# 30

# Down a New Road

Clad in jogging clothes and comfortable shoes Norm and I strutted briskly through the streets of Versailles. This early morning exercise routine had become a favorite time to discuss whatever was on our hearts and minds—our grown children, some insight gleaned in our devotions that morning, the soon-to-arrive house guests or problems and responsibilities in the Cambodian church.

The morning air was invigorating and we felt strong and healthy, totally unaware that soon we would approach the dread valley of the shadow of death. By our own calculations we still had at least 10 years to serve the Lord in France. Still, we knew we were approaching a change of direction.

This particular morning Norm again introduced the subject of our future.

"Honey," he said, "I'm sure that now is the time the Lord wants us to turn the Boulogne Cambodian Church over to Pastor Sopheap. A missionary isn't supposed to be the pastor of a church forever. It is time they had a Cambodian pastor and Sopheap will do a good job."

I agreed that Sopheap was well-equipped and capable. For eight years he had been Norm's assistant. He had taken many Bible courses and had been apprenticed in every area of the ministry. He also had spiritual insights into the needs of his own people and he was soon to be ordained. It was not Sopheap's qualifications that were a problem to me.

My question voiced again that day to Norm was, "But what will we do after you are no longer the pastor of the church?"

"I don't know. The Lord hasn't told me yet," was Norm's perennially frustrating reply.

I wanted to see farther down the road but God was asking for our obedience in just this one step. We chose to obey and gradually His plan began to unfold.

Since coming to France 10 years previously we had never taken the opportunity to seriously study French. Now having resigned the church this seemed like the perfect time to do it. There was a good language school in a suburb of Paris. We tried to enroll but our prayers and efforts were in vain. The door remained firmly closed.

Then another door, much more pleasureable, opened as we enrolled in the missionary language school in the beautiful mountain town of Albertville. Albertville was so far from Paris that no one from the Cambodian church could call on Norm for advice. That was good for everyone concerned—the new pastor, the congregation and Norm himself.

In this quaint little town we studied diligently long into the night and early in the morning yet the experience seemed like a vacation. We were free from the responsibilities of the church and, living in a sparsely furnished apartment, we were not encumbered by many things. And more, studying with young missionaries the age of our own children was rejuvenating.

The scenery was breathtakingly beautiful in Albertville. We immediately decided that since our work was studying and we did not work on Sunday that we would spend Sunday afternoons driving in the mountains. Each week we chose a new route and as the seasons changed so did the view. We would pop a praise cassette in the player and enjoy an audiovisual worship experience with each journey.

We returned to Versailles six months later feeling unmuzzled linguistically but no nearer to a knowledge of what our future would hold. Our Guide, however, knew exactly what He was planning. The groundwork for a new Cambodian church was already being laid in Marne la Vallee, a suburb 20 kilometers east of Paris.

Norm and I were excited about the possibilities of this new area. The beautifully landscaped parklands surrounding numerous small lakes made it seem almost idyllic. The streets were filled with Asians and small shops offering every kind of Oriental food catered to their desires—the perfect place to start a Cambodian church.

"We can still live in Versailles even though we work in Marne la Vallee," we assured each other as warm thoughts of our home and the precious memories it contained tumbled over each other in our minds. But we had not made the trip many times before we realized how impractical such an arrangement would be. Once again we would have to move. Just the thought of it brought tears to my eyes.

Finding a new place to live is never easy in Paris and its suburbs. As we prayed about a new home we asked the Lord to lead us directly to the one He wanted us to have. I made a list of all the things I would like or thought we need-ed so we would recognize "our" house when we saw it. A certain unessential item simply reflect-ed my heart's desire—a garden.

One morning we stopped at a rental agency.

"I have only one apartment of the size you are looking for," the agent told us. "There are no houses at all."

We looked at the apartment. I especially took note of a room near the door and smiled as I remembered a dream I had just a few nights before. In my dream we were in our new home and there by the front door was Norm's study. The agent showed us the living room, kitchen and bedrooms. Then gesturing outside she pointed at the answer to my unspoken prayer—a little garden.

We probably should have recognized immediately that this was the home the Lord had prepared for us but we thought we should at least consider the possibility of others. We phoned 12 other rental agencies in the area. Every one gave us the same answer: "Nothing available."

In October 1989 we moved into 10 Allee Britannicus with the certain knowledge that we were in exactly the place God had provided for us. And the small but loving Cambodian congregation became both our responsibility and delight.

# 31

# "*Even to the End*"

In 1990 we welcomed David and Yeang and little Jesse to join the missionary team working in the Paris area and just a few months later they were blessed by the addition of baby Stephanie. For missionary parents to have children and grandchildren living close by is a rare privilege.

Stephanie was only one of our new grandchildren that swelled the ranks of the Ens family during 1990 as each of our four children had babies one after another within five and a half months. Talk about multiplied joy! We even got to hold each one of them in our arms—another rarity for missionary parents.

In February of the following year Norm had the privilege of making another trip to Cambodia. With doors of opportunity for ministry opening once again it was a wonderful experience to meet with church leaders who had just recently been granted liberty to preach the gospel.

Norm's dear friend, Yong Soth, with whom he had worked 16 years before was now the president of the fledgling evangelical church.

And there were others who having endured the indescribable sufferings of the intervening years had emerged with their faith not only intact but strong and pure. Their loving welcome touched Norm deeply.

On his last day in Phnom Penh he met with 70 church leaders, some of whom were in serious conflict with each other. The Lord led Norm to share with them Jesus' last words from John 17, urging them to be united in love. As he stood before them no one suspected that this tender admonition would be the last words he would ever give them.

During his absence a special bond grew between us as I prayed for the success of his trip. He returned with good news of answered prayer and with some beautiful love gifts for me: a huge bouquet of Thai orchids and an exquisite necklace of freshwater pearls. We had missed each other and there was an extraordinary tenderness in our relationship during the following weeks.

While Norm was in Cambodia our daughter Shelly, a missionary in Côte d'Ivoire, Africa, had an unusually vivid encounter with the Lord as the Holy Spirit probed the depths of her heart one morning in her quiet time.

"Shelly, do you want My will even if it means someone in your family will have to suffer?" the Lord asked.

Shelly had long ago committed her life to doing God's will. *Why this question now?* she wondered. She was aware that a glib answer would not suffice so she postponed thinking about it. Somehow she sensed it involved death and she shrank away from the implications of what that could mean.

Finally she responded, "Yes, Lord! If you want to take my husband or one of my children, it's all right. I want Your will."

In the inexplicable way the Holy Spirit has of speaking to the hearts of God's children, Shelly realized that the Lord was telling her not that she would lose her husband or children but that her father would die. She began to weep and mourn as if it were an accomplished fact. As she grew calm again she wondered about the experience but assured herself that her parents were well and happy in Paris.

Easter Monday we jumped out of bed. We were on our way to Côte d'Ivoire! For months we had anticipated the joy we would have in visiting Shelly and Blaine (Sylvester) and their children.

We flew into Abidjan and drove from there to the beach of San Pedro, talking and laughing nonstop. For three days we played on the beach like gleeful children. Norm loved the big waves that came crashing in and at the end of each day he would victoriously announce that he was exhausted because he had stayed out in the ocean longer than anyone else.

Saturday morning, April 6, we helped each other pack and clean up before going to the beach for one last frolic in the surf. Shelly stayed on the beach with baby Adam while I joined Norm in the water. Grinning at me mischievously he urged me to jump the waves with him, assuring me that he would be there to help if I went under.

After a while I came out to hold Adam so Shelly could take a last turn. She had not even gotten her bathing suit wet when she cried out: "Mom! Pray! They are in trouble in an undertow!" Blaine and Norm had jumped a wave and suddenly found themselves unable to touch bottom.

Meanwhile out in the water Blaine assured Norm that it would be okay. They would just float a bit and the next wave would propel them closer to the shore.

"I can't," Norm said, his words jolting Blaine to attention. "You can go on without me."

Blaine noticed that Norm was not even struggling, but just moving his arms rather weakly. And the next thing he knew Norm's head went under.

Within seconds two medics who "just happened" to be on the beach reached him with inner tubes that also "just happened" to be there. While still in the water they began mouth-to-mouth resuscitation.

But Norm's heart had already stopped.

For the next 15 minutes or so they tried to bring him back, first on the beach, then in the back of the van and finally at the hospital.

The doctor said Norm had not drowned but had suffered a massive heart attack.

And so it was over, this joyful journey of nearly 35 years shared with a man of God.

# *E p i l o g u e*

In the days that followed Norm's death, I was surrounded with comfort and love. Since Shelly had been uniquely prepared by God for her father's passing she was strong to support me through those first sad days. I was deeply touched by God's kindness in putting me in her arms at that difficult time.

Norm and I had dreamed of another 35 years of growing old together, but God had other plans. His word to my heart was, "I am asking something very difficult of you but I am going to make it as easy as I can."

In Paris, too, I was surrounded by the familiar and comfortable and comforting. David and Yeang, Jesse and Stephanie lived just a 10-minute walk to the south of our home. The Hotel Climat where the Cambodian church met was a 10-minute walk in the opposite direction. As we grieved together Norm's congregation gently enfolded me with loving compassion.

And the Lord tenderly cared for me during the following 18 months in Paris as I mourned the loss of my husband. Our lives and ministries had been so intertwined. At times it seemed impossible to carry on without him.

But as time passed I came to the sad realization that my ministry in France was drawing to a close. It was exceedingly painful to say good-bye to dear friends some of whom we had known for years. But leaving the work I shared with Norm helped me to finally put him to rest.

I could not do his work then. I cannot do his work now. I can only do mine.

One of Norm's favorite songs begins, "There is a Redeemer, Jesus, God's own Son." We had sung it in church just days before God took Norm home to heaven.

Upon returning to Saskatoon, Shelly handed me Norm's sister's Bible one morning. In the flyleaf were written these precious words:

> *He is not only a Redeemer of sin but a Redeemer of our circumstances as well. He will not waste a single problem, a single heartache, a single tear. Our God is a Redeemer and He stands minute by minute before us, inviting us to let Him have the sorrow, to let Him have the disappointment, to trust Him to make something useful, something creative of every tragedy that darkens our lives.*

As I anticipate returning to Cambodia I expect my loving Guide to do just that. He will take the broken pieces of my life and with His creative genius He will make something different, something brand new and beautiful. I eagerly await the unfolding of His plans as I continue on this journey to joy.

*In the summer of 1994 Marie's missionary career will come full circle when she returns once more to Cambodia— another chapter in a lifetime of service to God and to The Christian and Missionary Alliance.*